The Way We Were Before Our Destruction

Lives of Jewish students from Vilna who perished during the Holocaust

Yulian I. Rafes

Edited by Paul Glasser

VIA Press
Baltimore, MD

with the YIVO Institute for Jewish Research
New York City, NY
1997

Yulian Rafes
The Way We Were Before Our Destruction
Edited by Paul Glasser
Copyright © 1997 by Yulian I. Rafes
Artwork © 1997 by VIA Press

All rights reserved. Except for brief quotations in a review,
this book, or parts thereof, may not be reproduced
in any form without permission in writing.

Published by VIA Press
Vestnik Informaion Agency, Inc.
6100 Park Heights Ave., Baltimore, MD 21215-3624
tel. 410-358-0900, fax 410-358-3867
Library of Congress Catalog Card Number: 97-60290
ISBN 1-885563-06-X

Dedicated to the
memory of the
innocent young victims
who perished during the Holocaust.

Preparation of the manuscript of the book for publication became a reality because of the creative and financial help given to me by two dear classmates
LILY MAZUR MARGULES
and
VERA SHAPIRO TOPER.
My sincere thanks to both of you.

I wish to thank the following financial supporters who made it all possible:

DINA ABRAMOWICZ
ANNA BALBER
RENA BIOXHAM
IDA GLAZER
MICHAEL MADESKER
GREGORY MAISSELL
ZENIA MALECKI
RENA MITSIOS
TEMA KAPLON
SOL KAPLINSKY
ANNA KREMER
RACHEL KOZLOVSKY
JANINE PACE
ABRAHAM SANTOCKI
GABY SEDLIS
TANIA PETERS
DANKA TURROW
TOBY WALTMAN
JAKUB STOLOWICKI

From the very beginning, the National Jewish Museum of Lithuania in Vilnius encouraged the author to publish this book and rendered him much assistance. Many thanks to them.

I was standing in
the Ponary Forest by
the horrible execution pits
trying to recall
the faces of my classmates.
I stood there and kept asking
myself, "Why were they
doomed? They were not
in any way different from
other students of their age
in Vilna. It may be because
they were JEWS."

                The Author

CONTENTS

Preface *(Dr. Allan Nadler)*	7
Author's Forward	9
Vilna — our native town	11
General information about the gymnasium (high school)	22
Students' self-help and its newspaper "Student Forum"	44
School life. Dreams about the future	67
Our class (III B) and those who perished	99
Those who survived or fifty years later	161
Epilogue	195
Appendix. Documents from Archives	199

PREFACE

The last generation of survivors of the Holocaust is rapidly departing this world. With it will disappear the last eyewitnesses to the atrocities committed against the Jewish nation. The survivors are precious not only as witnesses to the annihilation of their people, but particularly on account of the unique memories and experiences that they carry about the life of European Jewry before its destruction. They can instruct us not only on the lessons to be derived from the crimes and horrors of the Holocaust. Because of their unique experience of a rich civilization that no longer exists they can inspire future generations with the memory of a world of deep learning, simple morality and profound piety that has been tragically lost.

It is for this reason that YIVO is so proud to be the co-publisher of Dr. Yulian I. Rafes's unusual collection of memoirs, *The Way We Were Before Our Destruction*. This book distinguishes itself from the staggering quantity of Holocaust scholarship and literature that is currently being published in that it vividly describes the daily lives and mundane experiences of a generation of young Jews that never reached adulthood. Its focus is not on the history of the destruction of Europe's Jews, nor on the spectacular morbidity of their existence in the ghettos and death camps. By focusing on the simple, quotidian experiences of his pre-war school mates, by expressing their innocent frustrations and naive hopes, their childish enthusiasms and dreams, Dr. Rafes's book has the effect of underscoring how much humanity was lost, not with the stark statistics of the murdered millions and the horrific accounts of their deaths, but through a simple recreation of their young lives and hopes, as they themselves so simply and beautifully expressed them. In this book, for example, Ponar — the forest outside of Vilna which the Nazis transformed into the killing fields of tens of thousands of Lithuanian Jews — is also the enchanting forest of school field trips and picnics for young Jewish boys and girls before the war.

Composing this book has been a painful labor of love for Dr. Rafes, who has combined the skills of the professional researcher with the sensitivities and emotions of the world war II survivor. Unlike many other memoirs of survivors, Dr. Rafes did not rely on half-century old memories of events and personalities. He combined those loving memories with painstaking archival research in post-war Vilna, where he uncovered not only the many photographs of his teachers and classmates that appear in this volume, but also their very own words. He unearthed school records, report-cards, essays, and memoirs written by the students of his gymnasium, before they were so cruelly herded to their deaths.

YIVO is committed to documenting, teaching and reconstructing the civilization of "Ashkenaz" — the languages, literature, history and culture of our forebears. Our very purpose is to breath life into the vanished world that preceded the destruction. Dr. Rafes's work is unusually poignant and humane contribution to that effort.

Dr. Allan Nadler
Director of Research,
YIVO Institute for Jewish Research.

New York
July 1997

AUTHOR'S FORWARD

Dear Reader,

You are about to be introduced to the life of Jewish students in a school located in the ancient city called Vilna, known all over the world as the "Jerusalem of Lithuania." The time is the year just before the outbreak of World War II.

The sad and tragic feature of this book is that the majority of the participants - the teachers and the students of this school - perished during the dark days of the Nazi era.

I was a student of this school and when I used to think about the tragic fate of my teachers, my classmates and other students, unbearable and intense pain and sorrow filled my heart and soul. I used to ask: How could this happen? How can I forget my best friends, Lilka Rudnicka and Kuba Kuszkin, and what about the beautiful Niuska Kronik, in whom all of us boys were madly in love? Then I would remember so many others who are not here anymore. During all these years, I wanted to bring them back to life - but how? The only way was to write about them, describe their lives, their dreams, their potential to become doctors, lawyers, educators, artists. To show what was lost.

Many books, articles and documentaries have been written about the Holocaust; I have chosen a different form to express my outrage over injustice, anti-Semitism and racism and by the same token to pay tribute to the martyrs.

Let them speak for themselves! I will show you my school, my class and all the teachers and students, how they were before the catastrophe. In this way, you, dear reader, will comprehend the essence of this huge tragedy. You will hear their thoughts, their aspirations and their attitudes. I will give you just a brief description of the city and the school at that time, and then you will find essays, articles and poems together with authentic documents and photos.

Here are the three principle sources of my research material: <u>Photos and</u>
1) Documents (archival) about the school (Epstein-Szpeizer High School);
2) Documents about our class, such as: students' photos, examination papers, application for admission to the school, diplomas, etc.;
3) Articles and essays published in the school literary journals "Student Forum" and "Our Thoughts." Those authentic archival documents will surely illustrate you how their life was then.

While translating from Polish, especially the articles and essays, I have tried to be as authentic as I could and retain the thought and spirit expressed in them. They are written by thirteen- to sixteen-year-old school-boys and -girls and may often seem naive to us, but they are sincere, pure and truthful. They tell us about their lives, their ideals, their interests, and their attitudes towards friends, class, school and the world around them.

Look at the photos, those young, beautiful and carefree faces. Little did they know what was awaiting them. Just a short time later they were persecuted, lost their loved ones, were murdered and annihilated! There are no marked graves, no urns with ashes. As I consider myself to be their spiritual heir, their colleague, it is my moral obligation to present this book as a tribute to their memory.

May I now here express my profound gratitude to the employees of the Lithuanian Central State Archives Mrs. Milda Sheluynene and Mrs. Iren Paszkevich and the Book Chamber in Vilna, who gave me invaluable assistance in searching for the necessary material.

It is my very pleasant duty to thank the YIVO Instiue for Jewish Research, the research director of YIVO, Dr. Allan Nadler who helped make the publication of this book possible and Dr. Paul Glasser for editing it.

CHAPTER I

VILNA — OUR NATIVE TOWN

We lived in Vilna, which is now the capital of Lithuania.
In those days, it belonged to Poland. It is a town of old traditions. A lot of different cultures influenced the life of the city, Polish, Russian, Belorussian, Jewish and Turkish. Many hundreds of years ago Tartars, Karaites and other nations lived there. Vilna was always a source of friction, more often after the First World War, between the Polish and Lithuanian people. Each of them considered this town to be their own, and each of them was bound to it politically and culturally. Vilna was an apple of discord between these two peace-loving nations.

According to the Versailles Treaty, the town should have belonged to Lithuania as the ancient capital of that nation. Unprovoked, the Poles attacked Vilna and, under the leadership of General Zeligowski, conquered the town and its territory and made it one of the main cities of the northeastern Polish territory — Vilna Province. This had a big influence on the young generation. We grew up being influenced by the Polish language and the Polish culture.

Until the Second World War, Vilna was considered a very important cultural and religious Jewish center. No wonder that from the eighteenth to the twentieth century, Vilna was called the "Jerusalem of Lithuania." According to one of our outstanding historians, Shimen Dubnov, Vilna was a cradle of diffusion of light in many branches of human culture for the world. The first report about the Jewish community is recorded in the year of 1568. In the beginning of the seventeenth century, the Vilna Jewish community began to be an important center of study. In the second half of the eighteenth century, the cultural movement strengthened thanks to the activities of Elijah ben Shlomo Zalman, known as "The Vilna Gaon." This had a tremendous influence on all Jews. They began to publish religious literature. In Vilna, the house of Romma played a very important part in publishing and printing. They published the Talmud and other very important religious books. This house continues to publish even today in the United States and Israel. Till the end of the eighteenth century, Vilna was the center of religious teaching. The renaissance of the nineteenth century produced writers, poets and educators in Vilna. Vilna became a center of Jewish education. In everyday language, a "Vilner" meant a liberal man with education and knowledge. In 1847, a school was opened where future teachers were trained.

At the beginning of the twentieth century, Vilna became the center of the scientific movement in Russia. Yiddish and Hebrew literature began to flourish in the city. In 1903, Theodor Herzl came to Vilna for a visit. He was received very warmly by the Jewish population. Zionist leader Shmaryahu Levin was elected as a Vilna representative to the Duma (parliament). Among the many periodicals published in Vilna was a daily newspaper in Hebrew, "Hazman." A marvelous Jewish library was donated by M. Strashun.

The period between 1920 and 1939 was notable for social and cultural achievements by Jews in Vilna. During this time, many schools were opened for Jews: public schools, high schools and technical schools, as well as a teacher-training college, where the subjects were taught in Yiddish and Hebrew. Vilna was an international center for Jewish literature and culture and for the Yiddish language, with morning and evening newspapers. Many political, scientific and educational journals were published. The Jewish Historical and Social Anthropology Society was created by S. An-ski. In 1919, a Jewish museum was founded and in 1925, so was a Jewish archive. The Jewish Scientific College was founded as well.

In Vilna, such writers as Chaim Grade, Shmerke Katsherginski, Moyshe Kulbak, Avrom Sutskever and many more lived and participated in public life. The pioneer role in many facets of Jewish life was due to a subject close to my heart, medicine. Here, Jewish social medicine began. Here the world's first "Union of Jewish doctors" was created, and the first Jewish nursing school. Here, social organizations and institutions such as the "Society for Jewish Health" (OZE-TOZ) were very successfully developed. Much support was given to this society by Albert Einstein. Medical terminology in the Yiddish language began here. The first medical journals were published in Yiddish ("People's Health," "Stay Well," "Medical Articles"). Here, a hospital established at the end of the eighteenth century operated successfully and actively, as well as a hospital for poor patients (Mishmeres Khoylim). There were many more medical education centers, art centers, theaters, etc. In most of these fields, the leaders were doctors. Two outstanding names should be mentioned: Dr. Cemach Shabad and Jakub Wygodski.

There were many Jewish schools in Vilna, where all the subjects were taught in Yiddish, Hebrew or Polish. In the Epstein–Szpeizer Gymnasium, all the teachers and students were Jewish, but they were taught in Polish.

Alas, this Jewish life and its people were destroyed during the dark days of the Holocaust.

If you want to know more about Vilna, there are an enormous number of books and articles which describe the way life was there. On the pages of this book, however, students themselves speak about their life, their school, their dreams for the future.

This is the way one pupil from the eighth grade, Chaia Trewisowna, describes the city in her article "Vilna," one hundred days before she graduated the school:

"Vilna. Five letters. The whole word has been composed by a magic and invisible hand. For one man, it can mean something, for another man, it means nothing. To me — it is everything.

"From the very first day of my life, I can hear one and the same word. The sound of this word was different in different periods of time. Sometimes I listened to it light-heartedly, sometimes very much distressed, at other times — with sadness, sometimes with a smile on my lips. Sometimes it seemed to me that this word contained something very large, enormous, that has no end and cannot be placed within the limits of a human mind, and it also could seem, quite suddenly, that this word contained something very small, very dear to me, that this 'something' can find its place in my own self. Moreover, it has already placed itself in me and is planted in me very deep, deep and constant.

"I see Vilna differently at different hours, but always the same, nevertheless. At half past seven in the morning, I see Vilna with a stream of workers, aiming at one goal, but hurrying in different directions. All of them are alike, but so different at the same time: small, hunched, wrapped into the shabby clothes of their fathers. The heroes, those that dream about their breakfast at school — are elementary school pupils. Those who are children of well-to-do parents, are discussing books, cinema and theater — they are pupils of the secondary school (gymnasium). Whether with pale, exhausted faces or plump and well cared-for, they have one thing in common: they like their school life.

"I see Vilna with its open shops in Wielka Street, Mickiewicz Street, Jewish and Jatkowa streets and I see a road distinctly, even very distinctly — this is the road which I have been using for ten years, without interruption . . . Bored, upset, happy and with a smile on my lips; this is the road which leads to the three-story building that has on its gates the sign, 'The eight-year Epstein–Szpeizer Gymnasium.'

"This is our 'Marszalkowska' (the main street in Warsaw), the name which was given to Niemiecka Street by L. Alperovichowna. Our 'Marszalkowska' stretches right before my eyes. There is no time to get carried away by its beauty, for I am hurrying to meet my mother. At four o'clock sharp, I have to be at the end of Niemiecka Street. And I am already five minutes late. I am looking at my watch, distressed, maybe I will still manage to be on time, but barely.

"If it were another street, but . . . Bang . . . The stream of thoughts is interrupted by a mighty push. It is a somewhat old gentleman, who leaps out from the side street and falls down right on top of me. And a volley of reproaches begins, in which he scolds me and makes remarks about contemporary youth (and he does this in a tone that does not seem very respectful). After all that, I leave the battlefield, I am defeated. Now I have to make my run, and I am rushing in such a way that no one can stop me. That is why I am running like the locomotive of an express train.

"Stop. I am right on time. There is such a wall before me that it cannot be overcome. I get angry. I shoulder my way through the throngs of people and rush as Lincoln automobiles make. Everything disturbs me, and most of all, I am worried by the three ladies who are standing in the middle of the narrow street, chatting. 'Yesterday I saw a cape made of real polar fox.' 'Polar foxes? And I saw a cape made of ermine,' and so on and so forth.

"I pass these well-bred ladies and run ahead. In passing, I cast a glance at my watch and my hair stands on end. It is half past four. I am late. If I hadn't met so many obstacles on my way, maybe I would have been able to meet my mother on time. But the whole sidewalk is occupied by secondhand dealers, who are singing the praises of their goods. Ties, shoelaces, chocolate-covered nuts. I jump out right into the thoroughfare and run into a bicycle. I step back to the sidewalk again. To the left, to the right, these are the words I recall now, from a German story I have recently read. When I find myself in the place which was arranged for the meeting, it was already five past five. This

Chaia Trewisowna

is a record, I think. No wonder, because I went down our 'Marszalkowska.'"

This is what E. Oleinik writes in his article, "The Street":

"Different street peddlers, beginning with a ten-year-old children and going up to adults, are standing at the corner of Niemiecka and Jatkowa Street. They are standing in a row and shouting, 'Combs, soap, toothpaste and shoelaces. Only twenty groszy, not more. Today only and never again.' Or: 'The factory is selling out its famous perfumes at reduced prices,' and so on.

"Not far from this place stands a competitor to the state lottery, constantly reciting, 'Ten groszy is not true capital, everyone has to trust in his own happiness.' This is the picture of life around us.

"If a police uniform appears, everybody scatters as if by order and disappears rapidly behind the gates. As soon as the policeman steps aside, people appear in their places again, and commerce continues.

"You can notice a man at the gate of my house. He has a rope around his shoulder, and a small suitcase is hanging down from the rope. There are books in this suitcase, with fascinating names like: 'The Latest Fashions of the Season.' There are also different metallic badges, badges with different pictures on them, starting with a bicycle and ending with a butterfly and a school badge.

"I do not know who he is, I do not know his name, but when I pass by, I always watch him. Then he looks at me and says encouragingly, 'Will the gentleman buy something? My price will be cheap for the gentleman.' I see him every day, but I have never seen anyone buy anything from him. And at this very moment, while I am writing these lines, he is still standing at the gate and everyone can hear him calling "The Latest Things in Fashion. . ."

Morgensternowna, another pupil, writes in "The Symphony of the City":

"It is still quiet. The sleepy town is enveloped by the pink light of the sunrise. The golden ball of the sun is rising higher and higher, and everything is waking up to life. We can hear the lumbering sound of a cart, which was empty even a minute ago. A taxi passes quickly by. Soon students in uniforms appear. They are going either in pairs or by themselves, with earnest faces, talking in low voices or laughing loudly, gesticulating.

"Then, all of a sudden, the sharp sound of a siren penetrates the air. Workers are hurrying to work. Their steps on the pavement are monotonous and measured. Everyone is in a hurry. Adults hurry with dignity, youth — with a credulous smile on their lips. There is much

Emanuel Oleinik

hubbub in the street, the voices of newsmen break the typical daily street noise.

"The sun is getting higher. Now we can meet our mothers, who are hurriedly doing their shopping. The market is the center of all this hubbub, haggling and turmoil. Carts are rumbling nearby, "arbons" [in other words, the buses of Vilna — Y. R.] are passing by with a heavy grumbling. People are shouting, bargaining, singing the praises of their goods. Here a child is whining in his stroller, there a girl is weeping. Hungry children are playing in the dark and dirty side street. Then the traffic becomes slower, everything gets quiet. It is dinner time. It is getting darker. Street lamps and neon signs are gradually lighting up.

"Somewhere, the shop windows are lit. The life of this large city begins only now, late in the evening. Taxies are honking, the clatter of hoofs can be heard. Automobiles are whistling and loudspeakers are growling.

"A large wave of pedestrians pass by. There is a shout and laughter, and some fragments of the talk reach us from time to time. A gentleman at the gate is rubbing his hands over a box with handkerchiefs and calling out in a loud voice, 'These are the best linen handkerchiefs!'

"A young fellow, who is standing a bit further along, is shouting, 'Chocolate popsicles! Chocolate popsicles! Four for ten, two for five. Please buy, please buy!' But a mighty bass is trying to cover all those voices: 'Extra, extra! Hitler occupies Austria. The Anschluss! All Europe is in chaos. Only for ten groszy.'

"This is the paper boy, Valka, always drunk, missing one leg. An old gentleman comes up to him, he is looking through the extra edition very nervously. 'But Mister,' he says grievously, 'I don't see anything about Hitler here and nothing about the Anschluss.' Valka is hurt: 'And what of it? For ten groszy, you would like to buy the whole Hitler?!'

"And a bit farther, you can see window shops, tastefully decorated with colored paper. The windows are completely curtained. Is there dancing? Only the sounds of some melancholy tango penetrate into the street. There is a rich advertisement over the entrance, sparkling brightly. Multicolored little lamps are spelling out 'Cafe.' The colors are richly enticing. Suddenly, the advertisement goes out, as if by the touch of a magic wand, only to light up again, in a minute, slowly, bulb by bulb.

"Behind the cafe, several houses farther, we stop for a moment. Loud applause for a famous violinist is heard. Oistrakh reaches us, the violinist on a tour around all Europe now. When the applause fades away, you can barely hear the sweet sounds of the violin . . .

"But what does that shout mean? A large throng has gathered at the intersection. A fat lady is screaming with much emotion.

"'This rogue has stolen my last five zlotys!' Everything is in an uproar. There are shouts of 'Catch the thief,' the appeals of the victim, the policeman's whistle.

"Everything is absolutely different on another street. The largest park of the city is situated here. You can see a fiddler near the iron fence. Sad and quiet melodies can be heard. They are in unison with the noise of the trees in the park and the sighs of the fiddler. A policeman comes up to him and orders him to go home. But where should he go? Where is his home? The traffic gets less hectic. The advertisements go out, the voices are getting lower. The night is beginning to fall.

"It is already quiet in the streets. And only someone's scream and the clinking of broken glass somewhere in the side street can break this silence. And again silence, nothing important has happened."

That was written by Morgensternowna a few years before her horrible and tragic death in the Vilna ghetto.

Another girl writes:

"A hunched old man is passing by. There are a lot of wrinkles on his face, he is walking slowly, hardly even moving. There is much traffic in the street. People are in a hurry, pushing each other. The street does not know what pity is. Can this broken-by-life and crooked old man move them? Pedestrians push him, then go further, not paying any attention to him. The old man raises his head and looks ahead. How much does his gaze contain? All his life from his childhood up to the present moment. One look only, as if it is an attempt to riot, then he bends his head and goes further . . .

"Another old man is on Wilenska Street, he is standing and playing a violin. I do not know whether his playing is good or not, whether it is beautiful or not. But there is something in this music that makes you stop for a moment and listen to it. Such a sad note is always present. But even if he always played the most cheerful melodies, they would nonetheless sound sad, because the life of this old man is sad. This is how I feel.

"The street — traffic, taxis, buses are tearing away. People are passing by — old, young, children, they are sad, crooked, sinewy. Someone comes up to the musician, another goes away, someone is laughing, another man is crying. This is life . . . After the lunch break, people go back to their place of work. The work ends at six o'clock, and then the entertainments begin. Children are no trouble for their mothers. They spend the whole day in the open air or in lighted halls, under the guidance of experienced teachers and tutors. Children are being taught handiwork and other subjects. At twelve o'clock at night, the entire town is sunk into sleep. They are sleeping after hard work . . ."

V. Majzel, a pupil of the fourth class, chosen to guide a group of pupils from a Grodno secondary school who wanted to have an excursion around Vilna. And in his description we find his own perception of the city, the Jewish peculiarities of Vilna:

"We are now inside the building of the Jewish Research Institute (YIVO), where the secretary receives us very cordially and gives us a guided tour. We observe all the rooms, the huge masses of books and magazines, which, after they are put in good order, will serve as research material. We get acquainted with the history of the Institute, with its aims and its works, we visit the theater archives, we hold in our hands relics that once belonged to famous people such like Herzl, Mendele, Peretz and others.

"We have our dinner, and afterwards explore the old Jewish ghetto. Going up the stairs, we enter the old synagogue, in which every stone can tell you the story of Jews in Vilna, and every bench or lamp is a precious memory about ancient times. We look at the arc and the *almemor*, details of the crown of the Rodols made out of pure silver, the mighty iron doors that are four hundred years old, the legendary stone of Rabbi Samuel, the old lamps, and whatnot. And the old synagogue keeps all these things in its memory. Minutes of joy, minutes of distress were experienced by the synagogue together with the Jews, every inch of the ground here is washed by their tears, from the time of Khmelnitski until the present.

"We are observing the chapel from the eighteenth century, the one that contributes an important page to the history of the Jewish people.

"We cross the dirty side streets of the old ghetto, observing every place carefully, and we are possessed by a gloomy mood. It is very hard to get rid of that feeling [yes, Maizel, as if one felt that only a few years later, this place would be the arena of the greatest tragedy of the Jewish people].

"A short walk along Wilenska Street: along its gardens, we observe the cathedral from the inside and from the outside, and then we move towards the Zamkowa (Castle) Hill. From here. a vista of the whole city opens, we see the city, surrounded by forests and mountains, buried in greenery. We have been looking for a long time, and we cannot take our eyes off it. Only here, on the Zamkowa Hill, can one understand why Vilna has become the cradle of romanticism and the Jerusalem of Lithuania for the Jews.

"And the pupils of our secondary school love and worship this city, as do the majority of its inhabitants."

CHAPTER II

GENERAL INFORMATION ABOUT THE CH. EPSTEIN AND I. SZPEIZER GYMNASIUM (HIGH SCHOOL) IN VILNA

This Jewish secondary school with general educational classes taught in Polish was founded in 1921 by a math teacher, Mr. Ch. Epstein. It was a private gymnasium and its funds came from tuition.

Even before the opening of the gymnasium, Mr. Epstein organized courses that prepared students for the high school diploma equivalency examination. It is necessary to bear in mind that these were the first years of Polish rule after a five-year period of frequent changes.

It is clear from the letter sent by Mr. Epstein on August 10, 1921 to the Department of Education that he was asking "to postpone my concession for the preparatory courses until December 15, 1921. I can back up this demand with the following reasons: Because of detailed changes in the curriculum and remaining language problems, it is impossible for my students to take the exam in September [this is about the University entrance examination]. The University promised me that my students will be admitted on probation in October until January 1, 1922."

The first documents for the high school diploma date to the 1922-1923 academic year.

An interesting document that we found in the archives proves that from the very beginning, the owner and the director of the gymnasium, Mr. Epstein, cared a lot about the school's good reputation and was very strict about the norms of behavior for the pupils. This document is a petition to the Vilna Department of Education dated October 24, 1921, in which he announces the following: "On the twenty-first of this month in the evening, on Mickiewicz Street [nowadays Gedimina], my attention was drawn to the behavior of one young woman among several men. The girl was wearing the uniform hat of my gymnasium.

"I immediately checked her last name and found out that she was not a student at my school. Since I consider it my sacred responsibility to supervise the moral image of the youth at my school, I beseech the Department of Education to issue an order that the uniform hats of my school may only be worn by my students, and that these hats be sold only to those who show a student identification card. Uniform hats are white confederation caps with a letter G and an Arabic number that shows the class. Ch. Epstein."

Although the tuition depended on the student's grade and was between 220 and 500 zlotys a year, many students made discounted payments or studied for free. In some classes, there were from 8 to 27 such students. In general, there were about 120 students in all classes in a school year. The educational system at this time was: 4 years of grade school and 8 years of high school.

Upon the completion of the whole course of studies in the eighth grade, students had to pass the exams to gain a high school diploma (*matura*). Later on, this was changed. There were only four grades left in the four-year gymnasium, six grades in primary school and two grades in the lyceum with two departments: that of natural sciences and of social studies and literature.

As the minutes of the graduation exams in 1923-1924 show, thirty-four students took the exams. They took exams in the Polish language, Latin, algebra, geometry, written German, French. After the written exams, there were oral exams. Of the total number of students (thirty-four), fourteen passed the exams, eight passed with warnings in different subjects, i.e., twenty-two students. Five students were not permitted to take the exam and seven received exemptions.

Six people did not pass the oral exam. If we add them to the five students who were not even permitted to take the oral exams, the total number of students who did not receive the high school diploma was eleven out of thirty-four, that is to say, almost one-third. That is how strictly they graded knowledge in this gymnasium, and these great requirements corresponded to the high level of knowledge acquired by the students. The high school diploma exams went from 9:30 a.m. to 4:30 p.m. and were graded by a special exam commission that held a meeting after each exam. The commission was selected by the curator, the head of the educational district. It consisted of the chairman (usually a teacher from a different gymnasium), the gymnasium director and members who were specialists in different subjects, including the gymnasium teachers.

For example, the commission of 1931 included Ch. Epstein, Rubin Hart, Abram Fessel, Benedict Kostrinski.

There was a four-grade elementary school besides the eight grades of the gymnasium. For example, in 1928 there were 101 students in it: 48 boys and 53 girls.

As follows from the report of the school principle for 1934-1935, the elementary school improved the general level in the first grades of gymnasium. During the last years, the fifth and occasionally the sixth grades were taught exclusively by the gymnasium teachers. Because of the difference in the preparation levels of the students from the gymnasium nursery school and from other schools, it was customary to admit students from other schools to a special class. This method proved to be effective in balancing the levels of knowledge. Included was general Jewish education for Jewish children.

New students were never admitted to the eighth grade. As a whole, the student body was rather homogeneous in both school preparation and upbringing. In many cases, students were interested in specific subjects outside the mandatory school program. These interests were well backed-up by the pedagogical committee, which organized self-education clubs.

The problems of method of education and upbringing were usually discussed during the first meeting of the pedagogical committee. A detailed plan of pedagogical and educational work for the upcoming year was approved and a prospective plan that would include new needs of the gymnasium for several years to come was discussed.

The problems of upbringing were usually discussed during the meetings of the commission of class guardians. The link between the faculty and the guardians, that is to say, coordination of teacher and parent activities improved the level of the student's education. There was a total of 279 students in the eight grades, 139 boys and 140 girls; 92.8% of them received the high school diploma.

There were two libraries at the gymnasium. One was for students only, and another one for both students and teachers. On February 15, 1935, there were 3,544 books in the first library and 1,120 in the teachers' library. During the school year the library was visited by 186 students and 16 teachers [ISI-ARCHIVE of Lithuania, f. 172, INVENTORY 1. File 4538, page 8].

The library was open daily from 12 p.m. to 2 p.m. On a regular day, about forty-five books were checked out of the library. The library subscribed to five encyclopedias and thirteen magazines, including

"Teaching Physics at School," "Knowledge and Life," "Nature," "Historical Quarters," "Physics and Chemistry at School," "Young Technician" among others, and also several big editions, such as "Animals' Life," "Big World History," "Big World Geography." There was a librarian employed and all work was done under the supervision of the teacher of language and literature.

The pedagogical body was very strong.

There were seventeen tenured teachers and three substitutes. The director of education was Ch. Epstein, the director of administration was I. Szpeizer, and beginning in 1930, it was called the Epstein–Szpeizer Gymnasium. The administration included the secretary Charlotta Gerzer, librarian Leon Epstein, school doctor Doba Perelman, janitors Vincent and Eva Yasinsky and gardener Michal Matskyalo.

At different times, the following teachers worked at the gymnasium: Neti Sobelsonowna, Cipa Kaganowna, Rose Baum-Landaowa, Usha Epsteinowa, Dvoira Kvaisowna, Mikhal Shlozberg, Vulf Gurevich, Luba Shapirowna.

In 1932-1934, our class was taught by the following teachers: Danil Adler (Latin), Sal Ilinger (biology and geography), Abram Fessel (math), Chaim Gliot (gym), Ruvin Hart (history), Benedikt Kostrynski (physics), Shimon Meltser (German), Michal Morgenstern (Polish), Yudel Pomocnik (Jewish history, Hebrew), Sofia Wolkowna (labor education, art).

One of the facts that proves the very high level of the teaching body in general and of the teachers in our class more specifically, is that our school was often used as a practice venue for student-teachers. In 1933-1934, for example, there were six of them. Their master teachers were Kostrinski, Fessel, Ilinger and Hart. All of them graduated from Vilna University, many teachers had master's degrees in philosophy, math, one had a master's in botany and another in history.

So who were they, those whom we respected, loved, of whom we were afraid, whom we sometimes hated (mostly when they gave us bad grades)? What kind of life did they lead?

We have decided that it is better to let them speak for themselves and the following are some of their autobiographies. Of course, they were written before the war.

We managed to find these autobiographies in the archives.

Michal Morgenstern
Teacher of Polish language and literature

He was born on the seventh of May, 1899, in the village of Perpilovka, Ternopolsky region. His father was a clerk in a brewing factory and died at the age of thirty-three. His mother depended on her children financially, and his wife took care of the household. He had two children. His daughter, Cecilia Morgenstern, was one year older than we were and his son, Henrik, who was born in 1932, was also a student. He had two sisters and one brother who lived in Austria and in 1938 emigrated to Palestine. He was fluent in Russian, German, Polish, Hebrew and he could write in Russian, German, and Polish. He knew a little bit of conversational Lithuanian and Ukrainian, but his written skills in Hebrew were rather weak. He was mostly interested in philology and pedagogy, but was also qualified as a librarian.

He had a master's degree in philosophy and was qualified as a secondary school teacher. He spent his childhood in an abandoned village far away in western Ukraine and studied at home, supervised only by his older sister. Because of a lack of money, he only went to school for three years (third, fourth and fifth grades in the gymnasium). In all other grades, he passed examinations without attending lectures. He graduated from gymnasium in 1917 and was immediately mobilized. He served in the Austrian-German army for one year. In 1919 he accepted a job as a teacher in a small borough in the Avgustovsky region and worked there until 1921. For three years, he could not enter the University because only those who had been volunteers in the Polish army were admitted. Only in 1921 was he able to enter the department of humanities and the same year he got a job as a teacher in Vilna, in the Epstein–Szpeizer Gymnasium, where he worked until June 1940. In spite of many difficult responsibilities at school (he worked 12-13 hours a day), he used to study at night, and he passed two state examinations even though he hardly ever went to university, due to the lack of time. This he wrote on September 27, 1940. And in 1943, after the liquidation of the Vilna ghetto, Morgenstern was sent to the camp in Estonia where he buried the bodies of people shot down by the Nazis. Later, they killed him, too.

Morgenstern was a brilliant teacher of Polish language and literature. He was also a very delicate person, and everyone in our class and in school loved him. He was tall, slim, had a smart appearance and was in love with what he taught. This is the way we will always remember him.

Benedikt Kostrynski, teacher of physics and chemistry.

"I was born in Warsaw in 1879. I received my high school diploma in 1899 from Warsaw Real School. After passing an exam in 1900, I was admitted to the chemistry department of Warsaw Polytechnic Institute. I graduated in 1905. In 1907, I was offered a position as a math and physics teacher in the Vilna Gymnasium of P. I. Kagan. This gymnasium was evacuated to Ekaterinoslav in 1915, due to the first imperialist war, and I continued to work there until 1918. In 1918, the gymnasium was nationalized and I continued my career in pedagogy in the Soviet Labor School. On July 15, 1920, I was transferred to the First Ekaterinoslavskaya Soviet Labor School named after K. D. Ushinsky as a teacher of math, physics, and chemistry. On June 1, 1921, I was elected vice-director by the pedagogical board. Unfortunately, in December 1921, I had to quit working and go back to Poland. My mother was seriously ill and she insisted on my coming back. She died soon after my arrival. When I came from Warsaw to Vilna, I started to work as a teacher at the Epstein–Szpeizer Gymnasium, where I worked for eighteen years, until 1940. After the nationalization of the gymnasium, I was elected to work as a physics and chemistry teacher in the Twelfth State Gymnasium."

Sofia Wolkowna, teacher of art and vocational education

She was born in 1894 in Lodz. Her father was a pharmacist and died in 1917, when she was eighteen years old. Her mother lived on her and her sister's income. Her sister was also a teacher. She graduated from the Vilna Gymnasium in 1912 and from Vilna University in 1928. She knew Russian, Hebrew, Polish, German and French very well and she had some knowledge of Lithuanian and English. She had a gift for crafts. She was qualified in vocational skills (processing of wood, metal, glass, cardboard articles, bindery).

She started to work in 1918 in the Jewish Real Gymnasium, and from 1923 to 1940, she worked in the Epstein–Szpeizer Gymnasium as a teacher of arts and vocational skills labor. She also taught in the teacher's seminary. Her teacher's diploma was issued by the Vilna University in 1930.

She taught boys joinery. We had studios at school. The classes were run very actively. She was a petite, fragile woman, but how much time she spent with us, how much she used to put in! I still remember her conversation with me, I was class president then. "Rafes, I will write to your parents about your behavior." And I responded through

Benedikt Kostrynski

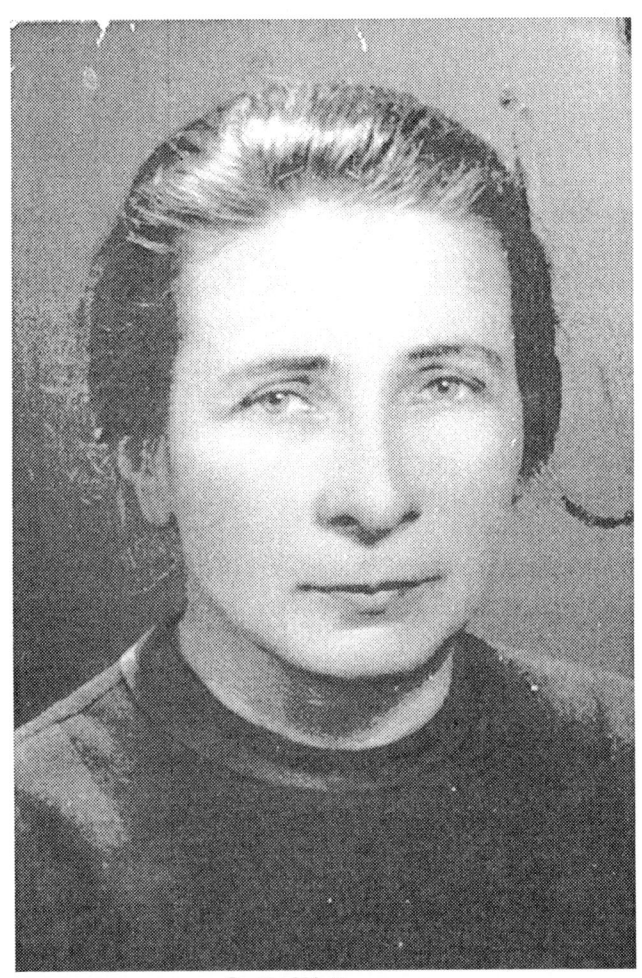

Sofia Wolkowna

clenched teeth. "Go ahead, write the postcards!" That's how it was. I do not know her fate, she probably passed away.

Yudel Pomocnik

Yudel Pomocnik was a teacher of religion and ancient Hebrew. He was born in Vilna and received his high school diploma from the Epstein–Szpeizer Gymnasium in 1923. In 1928, he received a master's degree in math at Vilna University. He received a teaching certificate at the University in 1931.

Frankly, most students in our class did not believe that they would ever use Hebrew in their life (unfortunately, they were right, but for quite a different reason). That's why they behaved very frivolously in class and did not study hard. Pomocnik was a kind and calm person, but he was not very good at keeping up discipline in class. His nickname was "mops" (bulldog). The mother of one of the students got used to hearing "mops-mops" at home from her son all the time. Once, at the end of the semester, she came to a school meeting, came into the classroom and asked the teacher in Hebrew: "Mr. Mops [Bulldog], how is my son doing?" It was really very awkward, and the story was passed from one generation to another, told by older kids to the younger ones. Yes! We did not appreciate our "mops," although the subject he taught deserved the highest respect and attention on our part. Too late. We cannot beg for forgiveness. He is dead.

Einlinger, biology teacher.

Einlinger was a teacher of biology, natural sciences and the head of our class. He organized the tours and traveled with us from Vilna to Warsaw to Cracow to Zakopane. He organized and headed the second tour in 1939, several months before the war. The itinerary was "Vilna-Grodno-Suwalki-Augustow Lake-Bialystok-Brzesc-Beloweska pusha." Those were unforgettable days.

If weather permitted, Einlinger liked to have classes in our school garden. There were benches and a teacher's table built there for that purpose. We very much enjoyed these lessons in the open air. The soul somewhat gained its freedom. The tours and the lessons outside undoubtedly merit the pedagogical talent of Einlinger. Maybe that was the reason why our class was so cohesive and kind to one another.

He survived, and after the war, he lived in Israel. He died there.

Chaim Gliot, the gymnastics teacher.

This is what he wrote about himself: "I was born in 1895. My

Yudel Pomocnik

father was a watchmaker and he died when I was one-and-a-half years old. My mother, who was left alone with two kids (my sister and me), could barely earn a living. At the age of fifteen, I went to Warsaw and started to work at a watch warehouse, where I worked until the beginning of the World War. I came back to Vilna in 1914 and found a job in the lumber business. At the same time, I continued with my education, and in 1916, I passed the seventh grade examination at a private gymnasium. I was very young when I became interested in sports. I was always a member of private gymnastics clubs in Vilna and Warsaw. Since 1916, I have been working at a sports club, 'Globus.' In 1931, I passed the state examination at Vilna University and was qualified as a sports teacher."

Gliot was a nice and kind person. He loved his job and we loved him. He was killed during the war.

Meltser, German language teacher

He had a nickname, "sipfon" (Seltzer bottle), because he was tall and obese. He was a German-language teacher. As far as I remember, he lived in Germany, and when Hitler threw out all Jewish citizens of Poland who permanently resided in Germany, he came to our city and to our gymnasium. I remember how he taught the correct pronunciation of German words. For example he paid special attention to the pronunciation of the word "I" - "Ich" in German. He used to say that it must sound very soft. Another word to which he paid special attention was the word "nebensetze." One can really appreciate his teaching methods from the following example. Twenty years later, in 1956, I had to take a German language exam for my master's degree. I did not study for the exam at all, and not only did I pass it with an excellent grade, but the examination committee especially noted my pronunciation when I was reading the texts.

A. Fessel, mathematics teacher

He was the most terrifying teacher, and when he called on someone, that student was horrified. He survived, moved to Israel, lived there for many years and died in his eighties in Jerusalem.

He was very pedantic, severe but fair. The main moment that used to put us all in a state of trepidation and tense expectation during class, was the minute he took a small notebook out of his pocket. He would peer into the mystical (to us) pages and start looking through them. Everything froze. Finally, like thunder in a clear sky or like a

Ch. Gliot

A. Fessel

bomb from a cannon that falls among soldiers, his voice fell among the students, calling "Rafes" or "Santotsky" or "Rudnitska," etc. All students at the gymnasium will forever remember this notebook.

Ruvim Hart, history teacher

This is what he wrote about himself. "I was born in 1896 in the village of Naguzhanka in western Ukraine. I finished grammar school in a borough called Yagelnitsa and in 1908, I moved to Ternopol, where I went to gymnasium and at the same time earned my living by giving lessons. During the World War, our whole household was ruined and in July 1917, I was called to join the Austrian army. I was there until November 1918. I was at different fronts, mostly on the Italian front, and there I was wounded twice. After the war, we slowly restored the household and in 1920, I began to study history, geography, and Polish language and literature in Lvov.

"During the whole school year, I earned money giving private lessons and often helped my parents.

"After I passed the examination in 1924, I got a teaching position in the Gymnasium of the Pedagogical Society and in 1926, I began to work at the Epstein-Szpeizer Gymnasium. At the same time, I was a teacher at the Teacher's Seminary of Dr. Charna for six years and after his death, I was the director of the Seminary for almost a year.

"During the years of teaching, two events made my life miserable. In 1924-25, I had a conflict with the teacher's union. In 1934, I unmasked someone who worked for the national security department and who relied on money that was coming from dirty sources. He tried to demoralize Jewish society. Despite the fact that this person partially pleaded guilty, the regional court did not permit me to submit enough proofs of his crimes and I was sentenced for six months and had to pay two thousand zlotys. That person was completely compromised. I was deprived of work for half a year. During all of the sixteen years that I worked, I supported my parents financially. Besides, I helped my numerous relatives and I also helped them to gain a higher status in society."

Hart's lessons were very interesting and fascinating. We were a little bit afraid of him because he used to worm himself into our confidence. It is not a coincidence that they used to say about him: "Not all dogs are harts, but all harts are dogs." This is because his last name meant a breed of dogs. He gave us a lot of knowledge, we loved history and knew it well. He, too, was killed.

Ruvim Hart

Principal, Chaim Epstein

Chaim Epstein was born on October 7, 1891, in Magilnitsi in Tarnopol County. He held a qualification as a mathematics teacher in non-specialized middle schools and teacher's seminaries with classes run in Polish.

He was tall, handsome, stern. We were really afraid of him. He was a retired captain of the Polish army who managed to escape during the siege. He was stern, but he was probably a brilliant administrator.

I met him only once face-to-face, but I still remember this meeting. After Abrashka Santocki and I disrupted the lesson with our phenomenal joke with barking dogs, we were called to his office. To be honest with you, I was not calm and cheerful when I entered the principal's office.

I opened the door. Right in front of me, in the depths of a long room, was a big table and at the table, HE was sitting; terror for everybody, the principal of the gymnasium.

"I am Rafes. The Principal called me." I said it very timidly and in a low voice.

"Yes! Tell me, Rafes, you are the class president. Who organized this dog's barking? This student has to be punished. You know this. If you do not tell me, you will be expelled from the gymnasium. That would be a shame for your parents, who are so respected in the city."

"I don't know," I said.

"Are you sure?"

"Yes," I repeated in a whisper.

"Then you are expelled until you remember!"

This is the way Epstein was. Of course, I did not name anybody. I spent three weeks at home not studying, until due to the energetic efforts of my parents, I was readmitted, to my own joy and that of my classmates.

Chaim Epstein, our beloved director, survived the Holocaust together with his wife and daughter Regina. His son Diunek, a student in our gymnasium, perished at the hands of the Nazis. They settled in Canada. Regina, also a student of our school, shared her memories of our director:

"Hands, large. Masculine fingers. Long and shapely. Gently tender.

"The child's earliest memory of hands is in a sun drenched room.

Chaim Epstein

She is attempting to walk by holding onto his outstretched middle fingers.

"The photograph is faded. The edges yellow. The moment long since receded into the history of personal trivia. A fragment out of the past, heavy with effort and sharpened by the clash of conflicting desires.

"The girl is fascinated by the motion of her own white shod feet which move clumsily across the reddish floor of the nursery, beguiled by the kindly gray eyes twinkling at her from the immense height of a tall being called Daddy. The child wants to watch both his eyes and her booties, but when she does, she falters. Time after time, she hits the floor with a soft, pulpy thud, her bottom protected by the padding of a linen diaper and a father's quick hands.

"Across half a century, from the forgotten crevices of the past, an image flashes with laser clarity.

"The girl sits on Daddy's knee. It's summer, somewhere in the country. Daddy is reading to her from her very own copy of 'Plomyczek,' a magazine for children, which arrives every month from Warsaw, shrouded in mystery, the faraway capital, the residence of Marshal Pilsudski.

"The child likes the stories from the magazine, loves watching Daddy turn the pages with his beautiful white fingers. She loves listening to the soft baritone voice reading about the little girl who refuses to take a bath, or the boy from Zakopane who visits his grannie at Sopot, by the Baltic Sea. She remembers Zakopane. Mommy and Daddy took her there the year before.

"Daddy insists that she take good care of her magazine. The pages must not show any signs of stains or tears.

"'Books are precious,' he says, his arms about the child. 'Books are to be loved and cherished. Even by little girls still unable to read.' He tickles her under the chin. The child giggles happily.

"In the beginning of each new year, Daddy arranges a special ceremony.

"Early in January, he takes the child and her older brother to a bookbinder to have the twelve copies of her 'Plomyczek' bound in a red volume, and the twelve issues of the brother's 'Plomyk' in green. Gold letters display the year and title of publication.

"In January of 1935, she will have three red volumes in the family library. On the inside of the cover page, Daddy puts a stamp which says, 'Ex Libris Regina Epstein.' The child is almost as proud of the stamp as she is of the book itself with its pristine pages. because the stamp states in Latin that the red volume is hers and has come from her personal library.

"September, 1939. The blue skies darken. Droning flocks of steel. Enemy aircraft swarm over the city. Bombs rain down on Vilna. To lessen the terror, the child sits at Daddy's feet, her head in his lap. His hands cover her ears. She is sure, well, almost sure, that with his hands against her head, no ill can befall her.

"Daddy, grey and shrunken, kisses the child goodbye before leaving for peat cutting at Rzesza. Her hand brushes the yellow star of David, now a symbol of degradation pinned to his back and to his chest right above his heart. Stigmata of the dispossessed.

"Daddy, no longer omnipotent. No longer young and handsome. No longer a source of security and protection. Daddy, stripped of the status of a human being. Prematurely aged, sad eyed, and sucked-in, haggard cheeks. It is this Daddy, helpless and hunted, whom the child loves with passion.

"Daddy's arms about her. The wedding band on his bony finger digs into her back as she clings to him in a final goodbye. The deafening thud of a softly closing door.

"'Look, Grannie,' says the child. 'See what happens when you turn the ball upside down. Look! The snow! See the children and the little house?'

"The old woman, the child of the thirties, looks at her Canadian granddaughter's toy. She nods. Memory, unwanted, springs into focus.

"A bitter cold morning in January of 1942. Escape. Daddy, now called by a different, Polish name, maneuvers their bryczka, a brown-painted wagonette, along the unpassable, potholed secondary roads which crisscross Poland like fractured veins.

"'Don't complain, Maria Regina,' says Daddy addressing the child by her new Christian name. The grey eyes smile at her through the frozen air.

"'These dreadful roads, the difficulties of transportation, all this is good. No police anywhere!' The child turns to look about the frozen wasteland. 'It improves our odds,' says Daddy.

"'Grannie, you eyes are watering! You have a cold?'

"'No, Darling. I just remembered something!'

•

"'I want you to plant a spruce tree by my grave.' Daddy dying of leukemia. 'A silver spruce. Will you remember?'

"'Yes.'

"She holds his hands, the lovely white hands with the shrunken skin and protruding veins. Tubes of blood hang from his emaciated arms.

"'Regina,' he whispers. His hands tremble in hers.

"'Daddy?'

"'Don't grieve. You have your own family now.'

"She swallows. There is no answer. She will miss him forever. They both know it.

"'I am sorry, Madam.' The voice is indifferently polite. 'This is the decision of the Appeal Committee. We cannot make an exception. Ease of maintenance. I am sure you understand. We can't have a spruce tree by any grave. There isn't enough space.'

"'Grannie why do you always stop by spruce trees?' asks the grandchild.

"The old woman takes a long time answering. 'It reminds me of a promise.' She swallows. 'A promise I made and did not keep.'

"'But did you try to keep it?' The child skips from foot to foot.

"'Yes.'

"'Then don't worry, Grannie. It's not your fault. Oh! Look, here is another spruce! You want to touch that one?'

"'No, my child.'

"'Then let's go, Grannie.'

"'Give me your hand.'"

In order for you to imagine exactly the state of our gymnasium during the last two years of its existence and seven months before the Second World War, let's look at the inspection report that was prepared on January 18-20, 1939 (S.G.A. of Lithuania; f. 172, l. ed.hr. 7063, page 33-34). Regional school inspector Dr. Balitski studied the minutes and the reports of the pedagogical meetings, clubs, magazines, essays in Latin, Polish, and German, math exams, homework of different students, and visited classes of different teachers. He noted the following:

"The school has many years of experience and follows its method of teaching in spite of all new tendencies. This inflexibility may look like a sort of conservatism, but this is only an impression. In fact, it just proves that the school has specific limits. The school does not approve of frequent changes among its personnel as well as in the educational organization. It tries to cut itself off from these changes because it is believed here that an important part of successful teaching is balance and calmness.

"That is why all new tendencies and views are accepted by the school with a great deal of caution and skepticism, and very slowly after numerous experiments and trials. Although if it does accept the new methods, then it guarantees positive results. That is why the pedagogical committee discusses pedagogical problems every year and they evaluate them from the point of view of being valuable and helpful for the school.

"The school has its own traditions and remains loyal to them as it tries to protect these traditions. New teachers either have to adjust to these traditions or to leave the school, because all staff members must hold the same opinions about education. The school principal does not approve of any dissonance.

"The school organization is very rational. This shows in both the way school is organized and in the way school discipline is regulated, with stress on the value of student's homework and the attitude towards parents' help.

"Students come to classes prepared for lessons and know the material of previous lessons well. The teachers pay special attention to it and they skillfully connect different parts of the material to create a full picture in the students' minds. This is worth mentioning twice because that proves that the students understand the goal of schooling. We collected proofs of this approach during the inspection in all classes. This was especially noticeable during the physics lessons in the fourth grade and during the biology lessons in the second grade of the department of natural sciences.

"Among the students of higher grades, especially in the lyceum, there are several students who definitely stand out because of their high level of knowledge and broad understanding of concepts. This shows in oral presentations and essays that are superior in content to what is generally considered a school norm.

"According to the inspector's opinion, the weakest was the first grade of the department of humanities at the lyceum. The teacher grades Polish and Latin well. According to him, the German language is weaker. The history teacher imposes very high standards for the youth and he gets good results. The physics and biology teachers also have good results. The organizational side is weak in vocational training and in art lessons. There is an obvious lack of discipline and the methods require a revision.

Upbringing. Special teachers supervise the realization of a prior approved plan. The students are taught that every delinquency will be followed by a punishment. The students are taught to be organized and responsible. This forms character, teaches them how to live in society and prepares them for future social tasks, for example, this is what happens in 'Self Help.' They also try to avoid cheap effects. However, they pay special attention to specific activities - shopping, help in studies, trading club, labor club, scholarships, different Friday clubs; they play ping-pong, listen to the radio, read magazines, collect a herbarium for the whole school, make presentations. However, the school does not overestimate the importance of all this and does not force students to accept an additional load, taking care of the student's recreation."

The inspector concludes that the "school work follows the plan and achieves the goal." This assessment of the inspector shows the style and principles of school work organization at the Epstein–Szpeizer Gymnasium.

During the years 1939-40, the school was called "the Epstein–Szpeizer Private Gymnasium of Vilna," and in 1940-41, during the Soviet era, it was nationalized and renamed the Twelfth State Gymnasium.

In the archives, we found an old balance sheet with the figures of teachers' salaries. All of the signatures were very familiar (although it was all very long ago). These were the same signatures that we often saw in our notebooks. According to this balance sheet, the taxes were from nine to twelve percent of the salary, depending on the wages. From these amounts, sums of money were paid in case of sickness and unemployment, which constituted the pension fund and labor fund, the rest were crisis tax and income tax.

This is the way our teachers were, the way our school was. It was definitely a good school. A school that cultivated honesty, fairness, democratic values, love for one's own people and respect towards other nations. The best proof of this is the material about school life that was submitted by the students themselves.

CHAPTER 3

STUDENTS' SELF HELP AND ITS MAGAZINE "STUDENT FORUM" (FRONT UCZNIOWSKI)

Students' Self Help

The student organization "Self Help" (Bratnia Pomoc) was especially interesting and original, and it played an important role in our school life. According to the documents that we found in the archives, on November 9, 1921, that is to say, during the first months after the creation of the gymnasium, school principal Epstein submits the following request to the department of Education. "Please be advised that the youth of the above-mentioned gymnasium has founded an organization called 'Self Help' for the youth of coeducational Jewish gymnasium with classes taught in the Polish language. This organization has the following goals: moral, financial and academic help to the youth. This organization is supervised by me and it has an administration of its own, represented by: Marik Solts, seventh-grade student, Rakhil Perelman, sixth-grade student and Samuil Berkman, seventh-grade student."

"Self Help" was a student's organization of the gymnasium and was based on the principle of democratic self-administration. It strove to cover all aspects of school life. Every student who could pay 50 groszy a year could become a member. The highest governing power belonged to the meeting of all members. Only at this meeting could the status of the organization be changed and the members of the presidium, i.e., of the executive power, were selected. They included a chairman, a secretary, a treasurer, a cooperative manager, heads of the sport sections and their vice-heads, a revision committee and a comrade's court.

Individual classes had their own organizations and elected the heads of their organization, including the chairman, secretary, treasurer, and sports and cooperative representatives. The chairmen of individual classes, together with the presidium of "Self Help," constituted the legislative body, called management, and they had a meeting once a month. Besides the sport section and cooperative section, there was a cultural club that planned programs for different events. Every Friday, one could read the newspapers and magazines in the reading room. The younger students listened to the older students, who read them interesting articles and stories. There were also several game rooms. The club program also included presentations with slides, plays, comedies, monologues, etc. Once a year, each class prepared a program for a club night. This was an opportunity to show oneself. At the end of the yearly club nights, there were literature programs and dances organized. We had very good time there.

An important role was given to humanitarian aid. For example, during the year 1935, the management of "Self Help" gave away hundreds of zlotys in emergency loans. Forty students checked out one hundred and ten books and manuals from the library. A middleman bureau that provided academic help, or help in finding jobs for colleagues-cooperators, was created. The school cooperative was created in 1934. It pursued the following goals: 1) giving away textbooks and writing utensils to students; 2) allocations for sporting events and excursions from their profits in the form of additional loans for non-wealthy students.

For example, there was a competition organized by "Self Help." The class that would spend the biggest amount on school supplies during a year was to get 35 zlotys back. The second-biggest spending class was to get 15 zlotys. This money was spent on excursions that were organized at the end of the school year. It is sufficient to say that during one year, the cooperative sold 1450 zlotys of merchandise and gained 350 zlotys in profit.

The purpose of the cooperative was that the students buy all necessary supplies on the spot and the profits gained by the cooperative be spent on students' activities.

In 1933-34, a sports section was organized. "Self Help" provided funds to get the necessary equipment. They bought skis and skates. They organized a skiing excursion and made a skating rink in the schoolyard, and that rink became very popular. On the average, one hundred and fifty students visited the rink. The hockey competitions took place on the rink. The sports section also organized basketball, volleyball, football and ping-pong competitions.

Our students took part in the athletics competitions among Jewish middle schools. Fima Klaczko took the first place in the 100 meters competition.

Sports champions of the gymnasium were Yuzef Dushtch and Shapsel Kamen. The whole school kept up with these competitions. Lilka Ferder took the first place in sprint. For the relay race of the 4 for 100 meters, the gymnasium was represented by two teams. Over all, the athletic team of the gymnasium took the first place in the competition among the schools of Vilna.

An important part of the "Self Help" activity was a cultural-educational aspect. Most important was a theater club that was created in 1929-1930. During a period of five years, the club staged twenty shows on different topics, including serious Jewish plays and reviews.

The shows were usually planned for such holidays as Chanukah, Purim, or for the yearly nights of "Self Help." The main theme and purpose was to present plays about Jewish history. They often staged the plays by non-Jewish authors, as long as the theme of the play was about the problems of Jewish history. For example, in 1929-1930, the club started its season with a play "Sholem Asch" (The Time of the Messiah). In 1930-1931, they performed "Uriel Acosta" by Gutskov. The school audience loved the play and it was performed twice. They also showed many revues of their own on Palestinian themes.

In 1933, with great inspiration, they performed "Daniel," a play by Wispianski, and it met with enormous success. The artists performed very well. Music, ballet, decorations, lighting, everything was on a very high level. In 1933-1934, they performed a play by Zhulavskiy that was written at the time of Sabbatay Zvi, "The End of Messiah." In 1934, they presented "Eremiya," a drama by Stefan Zweig. The following students especially stood out: Belitska, Oreh, Pruzhan, Komisar, Yutan, Epshtein and Mendel Shapiro. The decorations were painted by the students Aron and Peklyaver, and later, Yukub Shapiro joined them.

The management of the City Theater on Wielka Pogulanka provided adequate help in putting the plays on stage.

Clubs for literature and nature-lovers also existed.

All students were very happy that there was a skating rink, skiing, financial assistance, and excursions.

Printed School Newspaper
Student Forum (Front Uczniowski)

The first issue of "Student Dawn," the printed publication of "Self Help," appeared in April 1925, as a one-day publication. Then a new title, "Our Thought," was published in May 1929. In an appeal to

Yuzef Dushtch

Shapsel Kamen

the readers by the editorial staff, signed by editor S. Zalikson, it is pointed out that this is a collection of "our wishes," "our aspirations and ideals." "Our Thought" was young, healthy and crystal clear. For a long period of time, it remained asleep deep in our minds, not knowing of its existence, until we finally did bring it out and form it. There was an interesting article by a sixth-grade student, Geer, about books by Shakespeare and Wispianski, in which they condemn hostile attitudes towards Jews as unacceptable and a violation of human rights. There were poems, articles about self-administration, puzzles, and a recreation corner. Our teacher, Ruvim Hart, was responsible for the issue.

However, the first issue of this school newspaper also became the last one. In December 1935, it appeared again. It was published until 1939 under a different title. A sixteen-page publication of typed texts also included ads from different stores. In this first issue, there was an appeal to colleagues in which they wrote about life in the gymnasium and about the goal of the newspaper: "Only this year did we start publishing a newspaper of our own and here is its first issue. 'Student Forum' (Front Uczniowski) is our monthly edition, our thought, our flag, it is a publication of all schoolboys and schoolgirls from grade I-A to the eighth-graders to be."

This is how the editorial staff characterized the reader-colleague: "A student is not an automatic mechanism that memorizes conjugations and rules in hopes of getting a high school diploma one day, to make a career, or to go sweeping the streets. He is also a person who thinks and creates, who sometimes writes poems and essays that cannot be published anywhere else. These are precisely the articles and essays that he would put in his 'Student Forum,' in his newspaper, that includes everything that makes us happy and sad, and that no other newspaper writes about. In school, we learn cohesiveness, solidarity, and collective nature. Besides, the common fear of an F unites us. However, this cohesiveness remains inside separate classes, since it is a very rare case when classes cooperate. The newspaper should become exactly this type of knot that ties the whole gymnasium together. The section of reports will inform all members of 'Self Help' and the readers about everything each individual class has done during the month, how it worked and what it is planning on doing.

"Articles about the activity of different departments of 'Self Help' will replace the best posters and discussion articles about actual topics, and will give enough brain food to everybody.

"Even in our first issue, we have published an interview that will be followed by many other interviews. Humor is a big part. Healthy youthful laughter will not be put on the last page and it will not be an old calendar joke. It will spring like a fountain from many articles when we read about 'The Life of an Honest Student,' or a description of athletic competition.

"In this way, 'Student Forum' will reflect different problems that bother us, it will touch upon themes that interest us, will inform us about everything that has happened among us, students, and therefore it will become our publication."

This newspaper took an important place in school life. As P. Lewinowna writes ("Student Forum" #2, page 16), the first issue of "Students Forum" became a sensation and quickly sold out. Everybody talked about the newspaper. Everybody liked it. The students wanted to make a holiday, a free day in honor of the first issue of the newspaper. Unfortunately, that did not work. When the tenth issue of the newspaper appeared, it was cheered as a great achievement. Of course, the "Forum" had to overcome many difficulties. Those who write will understand what a great joy a member of the editorial staff feels when they manage to put another issue together and show it to their colleagues. And what about the pride and joy of the colleagues when they read their material published? "Student Forum" tried to be that unique and free students' tribune and the proof of its viability was the appearance of the tenth issue.

In the tenth issue, a student from our class, Y. Merlis, writes that during the last two and a half years nine issues were published, totaling 158 pages. In these nine issues, there were 219 articles: 51 memoirs and excursion impressions (23,3%), 42 articles about the life of students' self-administration (19,2%), 19 about famous contemporaries - (8,6%), 16 about class social life - (7,3%), 15 literature works in prose - (6,8%), 15 poem translations - (6,8%), among them from Hebrew - 5, from French - 3, from Latin - 3, from German - 1, 12 poems written by students themselves - (5,5%), 8 articles on history - (3,9%), 7 about literature and art (3,2%), 5 about books - (2,3%), 5 about social problems and politics - (2,3%), 3 about sports - (1,3%), 3 about movies and theater - (1,3%) and 7 on all other subjects - (3,2%).

There were 31 illustrations, three maps and two contests. During the years 1935-1938, a total number of 122 students wrote to the newspaper. 0,7% from the first grade, 16,4% from the second grade, 8,2% from the third grade, 17,2% from the fourth grade, 24 (19,5%) from the eighth grade and 34 (27,9%) from the first grade of the lyceum.

Merlis points out that the newspaper was very popular among the students and had a great influence on literary and self-administrative aspects of gymnasium life. And indeed, half of all of the articles were dedicated to school life and almost one-fifth were literary works of students, including poems, translations, and prose.

Therefore, the newspaper is a complete reflection of the school atmosphere from the students' point of view, and of their range of interests. At the same time, it is a valuable source of school history, it is characteristic of all parts of the whole schooling enterprise. That is why we used it so often in our work.

Talking about the goals of the newspaper, L. Kremer writes: "'Student's Forum' has to provide the field for the individual development of those who want to become better personalities. All those who would like to try out their own style and ability to express themselves will have this opportunity. They will be able to make known their ideas and opinions, to figure out the answers for yet unresolved problems and will help to improve the knowledge and intellectual levels of their readers. Besides that, 'Forum' is now providing the only existing and the most urgent possibility to unload the broadening, sparkling temperament of the willingness to explore that is youth."

Some people think that the Epstein–Szpeizer Gymnasium was too well assimilated. We cannot agree with this. Of course, the students were brought up to respect the country they lived in (this is obvious from the students' essays and articles in the "Student Forum"), but on the other hand, they always remained Jews and unfortunately, they too felt the anti-Semitic actions and reacted to them.

The proof of it are the problems discussed in the "Student Forum" and they clearly show that in spite of the fact that the classes were run in the Polish language, there could not be any real assimilation. Besides, the whole environment with its anti-Semitic emphasis, did not allow for assimilation. That's why it is really odd to separate Jewish youth of that time into "Yiddishists," "Hebraists," and "assimilators."

That was real life. One could either agree or not agree with it, but it was impossible not to take it into consideration. All this cannot hide the fact that it was a Jewish school with a Jewish environment among both teachers and students, and with a Jewish dream.

Many articles show it very colorfully. Let's listen to the student Zalkind, and to the ideas that he had about the fifty-fifth birthday of

Samuel Zalkind

Zhabotinsky (#1, pages 6-7):

"Vladimir Zhabotinsky is now celebrating his fifty-fifth birthday. This 'Spiritus Movens' of the Jewish revival shows constant unquenchable energy and activity that not every young person at his blooming age can show. Zhabotinsky does not get older and he is always productive and on the move.

"He greatly exceeds the borders of a publicist, orator, or a party leader. It is not enough for him that in each of the above-mentioned fields, he has reached the top. He contains something else that makes even an inveterate political opponent unwillingly admit that he is extraordinary. This is the most valuable part of Zhabotinsky's personality. That is that little 'something' that can not be precisely defined and that constitutes the miracle of this person, 'unique in his generation.'

"That is why our talk about the facts of Zhabotinsky's life, about his works would not reflect the full extent of his personality. The most important aspect is his position as a prince of Jews.

"Like a knight, he is a fighter and with his knight's arms, he is fighting against submission, humiliation, and lack of freedom of the Diaspora. He is fighting for the Jewish state, for 'restitutio in integro' of the Jewish people. Zhabotinsky always demands and appeals. He demands a decision, a reevaluation of values, a devotion, a striving for improvement for everybody from individuals to society.

"Not one of the outsiders uttered this without limits, and found more severe words of disapproval for the mistakes and vices of Jewish people in whose souls the ghetto is still alive.

"Despite this, in his fury one can feel the love for his people. He is a knight and a romantic at the same time. He has a great deal of compassion, pity, and understanding of those whom he castigates. That is why his fury astonishes, but does not leave bitterness. It makes one feel shame, but does not take the hope away.

"He is a romantic person, and his writing style is classical with short and precise sentences. His speech is made of steel, but he can also cry.

"After the horrors in Safed and Hebron, Zhabotinsky's speech was highly emotional. His torn phrases are full of meaning and reach the depths of the soul. An unseen secret melody carves its way. Everyone can turn the antenna of one's soul to this melody. Those who are able to will hear the music of our future.

"He is simple yet complicated. He is honest, but steady and firm. He hides his youthful love for his people under a mask blaming the crowd.

"Thanks to him, Russian literature has wonderful translations of Italian, English, and French romanticists. His spiritual food was Plato and Nietzsche, and no doubt he is the best topical satirist after Herzl. He is a spiritual citizen of both Athens and Rome, of Paris and Florence at the time of the Renaissance. He gives us an example of asceticism when he tears out of his soul this marvelous, wonderful, non-Jewish world, throws all gods from the altar and with tight, inflexible fanatic proclamations: a true Zionist does not have any other goal in life but the Jewish state. At the same time, Zhabotinsky is busy with philological work, Hebrew orthography and pronunciation, he reconstructs geographical names and he is creative and untiring in his great works as well as in his small works. Even when he was put into solitary confinement in Acre for organizing a defense during the Jewish massacre and was awaiting capital punishment, he did not tire of serving his people. He himself creates the 'history of the Jewish Legion' and at the same time, he is the monument to his spiritual brother, Trumpeldor, about whom the legend is building up.

"Zhabotinsky says that 'youth is not only an age problem.' Youth is a high title and it is not enough just to be born to earn it. A small number of years is only a mathematical part. There are underdeveloped, spiritually small dwarfs, but they are not young. To be young is to be able to revive in oneself the ideals of beauty and virtue, it is the possibility to fully give oneself to an idea, it is looking without boredom at the eternal stars.'

"In our gloomy world of economic messes and selfish goals, Zhabotinsky raises high the pathos of poetic ideals and a nation's culture."

The students were interested in events in Palestine. They used to discuss its problems and to propose possible solutions. When there were disturbances in Palestine, our student, L. Kremer, said the following: "What conclusion can we draw from the latest disturbances? These events proved that we cannot count on England, that we need to create our own armed force that would defend the whole Yishuv. Dying a hero in Tel-Hay, Trumpeldor said that a Jew who is building Palestine must be not only a farmer and a worker, but also a soldier. The latest disturbances clearly showed that the ideas of Trumpeldor should be implemented without any deviations" (#5, pages 9-10).

L. Kremer gives a detailed description of the disturbances in Palestine, describes positions of different groups and tells about the fight between the Arabs and Jewish settlers. As a result of the disturbances that were started by the Arabs, Tel Aviv obtained permission to build a port. But the main victory was that the Jews finally felt their strength. The Arabs realized that they could not just keep on organizing the massacres as they had in 1929.

The students not only thought about current Jewish life, but they also dreamed about a wonderful future, and these fantasies were often connected with their country, with Palestine. The student P. Dayhesowna gave the form of a dream to such a fantasy and today has become a reality. Let's listen to her...

"I hardly ever have dreams. And even when I do have dreams, they do not leave any traces. Dreams disappear from my memory and even with the greatest efforts, I am not able to reflect on them. This was the only dream in my life that I remember well. It was during the holidays of Sukkot. It was eleven p.m. It is deadly quiet in my room and only the ticking of the clock interrupts the silence. I am lying in my bed and reading a chapter from a magnificent utopian book by L. Balmont, 'The Promised Land.' The hour hand is trying to catch up with the minute hand and meet together at twelve. Slowly, I stop reading. Instead of words, I see beautiful pictures of this wonderful story. I start daydreaming. Suddenly, the book falls out of my hands. I turn off the lamp. The angels of dreaming close my eyelids. Good night.

"What a pleasure! Trieste. There is a lot of traffic and movement in the port. There are thousands of young people and I am among them on the passenger's pier. In an hour, we start on our way to Erets. The boat 'Tel Aviv' will take us there and a white and blue flag will be blowing in the wind. The whistle of the horn. 'Sit down!' One hears the voice of the captain. In a second, the pier becomes empty. 'Hakshev!' suddenly sounded in the air. Thousands of young bodies feel tension. The orchestra plays 'Hatikva' and the Italians salute. The boat quivers. It is departure time. The weather is beautiful. The landscape is charming, with a southern sky and light breeze. The ships in the port get smaller and smaller and look like toys. The front of 'Tel Aviv' cuts through the ocean waves. Everybody is happy on the deck. Songs, dances and songs and dances again and again. I dance and sing, but my thoughts fly far away to Erets. The boat goes forward fast, excited by the ravishing song of hope that the ocean waves used to sing to the exiles coming back after the century-long travels. Haifa. Huge crowds of people on the pier. Music, singing, and slogans stupefy me. People hug each other. Some people cry because of joy. What about me? My brother is hugging me. I start to cry. I do not even have a chance to turn around when I find myself in a taxi. Through the window, I look at the countryside. As in a movie, I see wonderful pictures of the kibbutz. Everything is covered by trees, grass, and the golden sunshine of the Palestinian sky. Fatigue seizes me. I fall asleep leaning on my brother's shoulder, and suddenly I shudder. A catastrophe. God save us all. It is my mother who pulls me by the sleeve.

"'Get up, my child, it is a quarter to six, you'll be late for school.' What? School? Late? Where am I? I wipe my eyes. Nothing special, only the 'Promised Land,' the cause of the wonderful dream, is lying on the floor." (#3, page 2).

Reading this dream some sixty years later, one is astonished at how this young girl could predict what was still to happen. But none of them could predict the tragedy that would happen to them all in a few years.

An all-honors student, Benjamin Mirski (one could not find many of them in the gymnasium), was interested in analyzing the works of Jewish writers and poets: Bialik, Mendele Moykher-Sforim, Chernikhovski. He translated Bialik's poems from Hebrew, and analyzed the works of Mendele.

According to Mirski, Mendele describes Jewish poverty with horrifying realism. He presents different types of ghetto, the characters and relationships in small towns. Mirski points out that the writer manages to present the pictures of the way of life of Jewish people, to describe the dreamy Jewish soul that is peering into the stars from behind the misery and swamp.

That is exactly why, as the author of the article points out, "We value the singer of the ghettos so much, and now, on the day of his one-hundredth birthday, we kneel before the greatness of his talent."

He comes back to the Jewish theme, and in the article dedicated to Saul Chernikhovski, one of the well-known poets who wrote in Hebrew and whose works are full of human universality, Mirski writes,"Chernikhovski discovered new horizons in ancient Jewish poetry not only because he enriched it with the works of world literature and so gave it a universal character, but also because he was the first to introduce the forms of idyll, ballad, and sonnet."

Striking in this analysis of old-new Jewish literature made by a sixteen-year old teenager is his trust in the future and in the perspectives that have only recently become a reality.

Mirski noted that the literature of the revived modern Jewish people with few exceptions, was created in Palestine and it is naturally connected with that renaissance. It tells about both the positive and

Benjamin Mirski

negative sides of the Yishuv and sometimes one can feel the echo of Diaspora. In the first place, this literature is imbued with the joy of life and optimism. This literature signifies the morning of new life, renaissance, and a healthy life style.

According to him, all new Hebrew literature is one great epos of the renaissance process in people and it proves that Hebrew has an inexhaustible ability to survive.

These gymnasium student's words date more than half a century back. And still, note how actual and modern they sound today.

The students were interested in the history of the Jewish people, in the Jewish religious life of their native city.

The student V. Maizel talks about Babylon and ancient Jewish culture, and he points out, "Almost two thousand years have passed since these tragic days when the Jews lost their statehood. Then the difficult period of their wanderings in the world started and it continues till today.

"The Jewish nation has suffered a lot, but has retained almost the same life force it once had. Other ancient people have disappeared, but the Jewish people did not stop being a whole nation despite all the humiliations, despite the fact that they were beaten up and scattered all around the world. There must be strong connections that unite Jews if in spite of brutal persecutions and massacres, they do not cease to exist and to develop. This connection is in fact our Bible, the basis of our existence. The whole civilization and political history of the people of Israel consists of the Bible. Besides its universal and patriotic meaning, it has the value of a patriotic document in which the people for centuries have been investing the fruit of their development."

This student decisively repulses the Nazi German scientists who contend that the Babylonian codex is more ancient. He writes, "The moral abyss between the Bible and Babylon proves that the Bible is a creation of Israel. It will forever remain a pride and glory of Jews."

He also did a very interesting analysis of different types of Jews in the synagogues of Vilna. This is what he says.

"Those who want to look at the exposition of Jewish types can go to their familiar synagogue backyard. There one can meet old, crippled Jews with prayer books in their hands and with talises under arms who keep animated discussions going by gesticulating.

"Here is a guide, crippled and trembling because of his old age, Rabbi Shmarye, who argues with everyone on every topic with the enthusiasm of a child. Another one with a nose full of tobacco and dimmed eyes is an interesting type of a traditional Jew. All his life has been spent on prayers and study. You can meet him at the synagogue every day. As a rule, he is sitting there by himself, absorbed in his prayers from sunset till morning. Then he goes home. He eats his breakfast of black bread with onions, drinks his tea and returns to the synagogue. There, everyone knows him. It seems that even the fretted walls and benches bend to him. That is not surprising. Most of his long life has been spent within these walls. These benches remember the times when he was still a youth. That's why Rabbi Shmarye feels better here than anywhere else. With others of his age here, he studies the immense, infinite Talmud.

"Enjoying himself, he plunges into this divine science, the only pleasure in his life. From it, he draws force, hope, and cheerfulness. Ascetic Rabbi Shmarye neglects modern life. 'Everything is nothing in this world,' he repeats the words of Ecclesiastes to himself. The old man's life is all in the hope that the Messiah will come. Only then will life in the Promised Land begin. And his sons are without God, they gave up the divine science and became unfaithful. One proclaims that the Jews with arms and labor must win the divine land and in that way free all Jews from slavery. The other one raves about the equality of all people and about other difficult matters. Shmarye says that because of people like this, the Messiah will not come.

"Samuel, one son of Shmarye, has a deep, melodic voice, not like his father's. He convinces everyone that Jews are a people with a rich and glorious history. Ill-fated rabbis plunged this exclusive people into darkness and made them a laughingstock of other nations. They believe that a prayer, of which they do not even understand the words, can restore the Jewish state. First, the Jews have to convince the whole world that Jews are still alive and in fact a nation. After that, they need to win Palestine back and rebuild it with their own labor. Samuel believes that a Jew is a person like everyone else and therefore has to dress like all Europeans do. This is also a reason for his father, who is against any nation, to be upset. However, his son believes that education and European culture are virtues for humanity.

"His other son is Ber. When Shmarye thinks about him, he sighs deeply. That one is a real renegade who does not even believe that the Jewish people exists because he thinks that all people are brothers. Shmarye used to hit his sons and tried to kick the devil out of them, but he does not have that strength any longer. And all his guilt is about education. 'Why did I sent them to school?' The old man sighs. Shmarye is only happy about his son-in-law. He is a rich merchant. He takes care of his business, does nothing against Shmarye's word and prays a lot!"

This is what Maizel wrote in the fourth grade. Here are magnificently grasped members of one Jewish family, all with different characters and with different ideals in life. This corresponds to the stratification in Jewish society. On the left are revolutionaries, Zionists, religious movements and those without an ideology, who only think about their income and the well-being of their families.

The youths in the Epstein–Szpeizer Gymnasium were not only interested in history, but also paid close attention to the activities of contemporary Jewish scientists and politicians. They tried to make contact with them. In doing so, they were trying to separate the most important and meaningful parts of Jewish culture from the past to the present.

The students familiarized themselves with the works of the main rabbi of the Warsaw synagogue, M. Shor, as well as with his research in Assyriology and Jewish history. They sent him several issues of "Student Forum." Mr. Shor responded, and in his letter we read, "Thank you for sending me the two latest issues of "Student Forum". The content of the issues is interesting and very diverse. It is also adjusted to the thinking level of older students. However, I believe that there must be a special section devoted specifically to the analysis of new research in Judaic (history and literature) that is published in Hebrew and European languages. It is also expedient to analyze the problems of religion. Please express deep gratitude on my part to the students and member of the editorial staff of this wonderful school newspaper."

There was information about Vilna organizations, museums, theaters, societies. Student correspondents were sent to those places. This is what S. Flaksowna said: "In order to familiarize my readers with the activity of the Jewish Scientific Institute, the editorial staff sent me to this organization to interview Dr. Max Weinreich.

"At the very entrance to this unusual building, we notice a big wall map that illustrates 16 million Jews spread out all around the globe in 1934. Next to the map are diagrams that show the activity of Jewish scientific institutes.

"I have an appointment with Dr. Weinreich, a well-known Jewish leader, and I have several questions to ask him. 'When and how was the Institute created?'"

"'The real date of the foundation of the Institute is March 24, 1925. The author of this project was the well-known Jewish leader, N. Shtif, who at that time was in Berlin. Other people implemented his

Sara Flaksowna

project. They were Cherikover, Reyzin, Lestchinsky, and others.'

"'What are the most important moments that one can note in the development of the Institute?'"

"'The Institute began from almost nowhere and within a few years developed enormously. The first meetings took place in my own private apartment. Soon, however, we got a room in a building at 18 Wielka Pogulanka Street. Then we got a second room and finally the whole floor. In 1933, we moved to our own building at 18 Wiwulski Street. In 1925, there was our first big meeting in Berlin and in 1929, the first conference in Vilna. A very important date in the Institute's life is 1931, when the first issue of "YIVO-bleter" was published.'"

"'What are the goals of the Institute?'"

"'The Jewish Scientific Institute must become a center for Jewish science and an organization that will elevate young scientists.'"

"'How is the scientific research organized?'"

"'There are four departments at the Institute: philology, economics and statistics, history, psychology and pedagogy. In addition, research among 16-20-year-old Jewish youth was organized. For this purpose, they organized a contest of autobiographical questionnaires. Besides the main departments, there are also departmental aids, such as a bibliography center, library, archives, and a museum.'

"Dr. Weinreich shows me a diagram that demonstrates the organization of the Institute. 'Clubs of sympathetic people join together in the organization of separate states and they send their delegates to the general congress. There they elect curators as a council and a central board of directors that in turn create an executive bureau. Members of the honorable presidium are Einstein, Freud, and Dubnow, among others.'

"Dr. Weinreich invites me for a tour of the Institute and I agree immediately. I visit a real labyrinth, including the theater museum, the center of the library, reading halls, underground stacks, until we get to the exposition, 'The life and creative work of Mendele Moykher Sforim.'

"'What do the library and the book stacks consist of?'"

"'There are 40,000 books in the library. Besides that, there are ten thousand yearly collections of Jewish newspapers, three hundred and fifty autobiographies, one hundred thousand songs, legends and sayings with the descriptions of folklore customs, two thousand projects that relate to Jewish theaters, authors and scenario writers. All of it comes from gifts and donations.'

"'What was the occasion for the last meeting of the Institute and what was the goal of the meeting?'

"'After almost a six-year interval, we had a meeting in 1935. The goal of the meeting was to report the activities of the Institute, to elect the new board of directors and to approve new regulations.'

"'It was decided to enlarge the graduate school named for Dr. Shabad. Professor Dubnow promised to advise graduate students at the history department. In order to allow young scientists to fully devote themselves to research, they will be given stipends.'

"'From what sources does the Institute get its funds?'

"'The funds come from the donations of different societies and organizations all around the world. The yearly institute budget was half a million zlotys. One third of this amount comes from the United States, Poland is second in funding, and then come all other countries.'

"'Does the Institute offer anything new?'

"'We have just finished the preliminary work for the foundation of the Museum of Jewish Art.'

"At this point. I end the interview. I thank Dr. Weinreich for his amiability and wealth of information and leave the Institute."

The above definitely had great positive educational influence on student readers. It raised their intellectual level in terms of national Jewish consciousness.

This is clear proof of the fact that the minds of the gymnasium students were filled with the theme of Jewish life. It also proves that there is no reason to consider the teaching of the Polish language in the gymnasium as an indication of an atmosphere of assimilation.

In the newspaper, reports about the activities of the students' self-administration were published. In the report for the first semester of 1935-1936, it says (#2, pages 10-11) that there were eleven meetings with a total number of 1490 participants. Educational clubs met 48 times and 545 people participated in these meetings. Membership fees gave an income of 197.50 zlotys. There were urgent assignations for the amount of 235.00 and 136.75 in assignations with no due date. The textbook rent office gave 111 textbooks to 43 students. Book rental was one-fifth of cost. Poor students get the textbooks with discounts or for free. The cooperative sold merchandise for the amount of 1551. 26 zlotys. It earned a profit of 537.63 zlotys. The first issue of "Student Forum" was published. The circulation was 380 copies. "Self Help" has a photo library and a camera. They take pictures during excursions and different activities. Every club meeting has two parts to it, a literary part and an artistic part. Yearly parties of "Self Help" have a slogan: "Every class has a vote." Students that have already graduated from the gymnasium and their parents are also invited to these parties.

"Self Help" did a lot to advertise travel. This showed primarily in yearly contests given by the school cooperative. The rewards received by classes were given in the form of subsidies to poor students who wanted to participate in the excursions. At the end of 1934-1935, it was decided to advertise the creation of traveling camps. The parents were against it but that problem was resolved. Seven female students, eight male students and two guards took part in this outings. They traveled for twenty days in the mountains, for sixteen days in the cities and industrial centers. They spent four days by the sea. They traveled 3,445 kilometers by train, 68 kilometers by bus, 92 kilometers by horse-drawn cabs, 55 kilometers by boat, and walked 365 kilometers for a total of 4,016 kilometers. Ten students have paid for the tour in full. Two students paid a portion of the cost. The camp was six weeks long.

Besides that, there were organized permanent monthly camps. This is how A. Feygin (#11, pages 4-5) describes his first day in camp in the "Novo-Sventsiani" region in Pimpelki:

"Look through the train window at different scenery. Always the same fields, woods and swamps. It is a tedious trip, but we are not bored traveling through the monotonous landscape of the Vilna countryside because we are going to the camp, the goal of our dream. In the car, we discussed what it will look like. Will our house be situated among mountains or in the aromatic fields? Will the roof of the guy's barn have holes and will there be horses and cows nearby? Some of us were upset because for a long period of time, we would not see our relatives.

"We form lines. Behind us is the Novosventsyanski station and in front of us Yudel and Mishka, our outpost. We walk up the unknown streets. Izka wails on his trumpet, Simka plays the second part on his drums. Everybody looks at us with great interest while kids ten years and younger march by our side and follow us to Pimpelki. Right by Pimpelki, there are large excavated land spots.

"We reflect on it. As these forests were uprooted to sow the rye, so all vices will be rooted out of our souls and altruism, fairness, courage, and collective nature will be introduced.

"Right after we put down the heavy backpacks, we prepared our mattresses and pillows. When everyone had settled in, normal camp life started. Some helped to prepare lunch, others carried water and wood, still others put up the flagpole. After lunch, Suli, Mishka, and I went to the forest to cut down several trees for the gate. What a joy! I hit the tree one, twice, I put my ax on the bark faster and faster, then I get to white lumber. The tree shakes. Another blow and the tree falls. Meanwhile, our waving light-blue flag with a lily stands out against the sky's background. After work, when we are already lying in the barn under the comforters, our great "first night" has started. That was not a night any of the guys would forget. That night, like all other nights, was meant to be a night for sleep. But who slept during this remarkable night? First, everyone wanted to talk about something important. The culmination of this night were dances. Just imagine someone holding a flash light dancing in his night gown with great artistry and totally forgetting himself. Laughter continues well after midnight until we finally fall asleep, very tired. The first day passed. The first night passed, then there were all the other days and nights like a dream or a fairy tale that leaves a deep and persistent mark. That continued for twenty-two days. However, it was quite a time in our life."

A lot of work was done organizing excursions to different cities like Warsaw, Zakopane, Narocz, Grodno, Belovezska forest, Augustovkie lakes, Lodz. These excursions were headed by the teachers Hart, Morgenstern, Fessel, Eilinger, and others.

Compared with the self-administration units in other schools, "Self Help" managed to implement much more. At the same time, it was criticized. For example, the reading room, which had fifteen different magazines and newspapers, was open only once a week, and students did not provide sufficient help to other students. Of significance in this respect was the criticism of how jobs in the school hierarchy were distributed.

Student P. Yakobuvichuvna (14 years old) writes in her article "Accusation" (Student's Forum," #2, pages 14-15):

"It is already 10 p.m. I am reading a very interesting book. I stop reading because one thought torments me. School life is very interesting, full of different events, but there are still things in life that make one suffer.

"You, my colleagues, are guilty of it because you helped in establishing this mood in school. You choose some students for numerous activities. You assign to them different offices and even several offices to one student. Isn't it an unfair system? Some are completely unknown and all fingers are pointed at others. Why should it be that way? Isn't there enough unfairness in the world that even within the school walls, something like that should be happening? There are some who would say: 'If no one had gotten selected, there would have been nothing in school. There would have been no sports section, no cooperative, no edition and finally "Self Help" would not exist and our school would not be worth anything.' To this I will respond, 'If you want to reinstate fairness in our school, then you should elect everyone in turn to the positions in self-administration. Let unity and fairness triumph in school. We have to stand by the offended.'"

In #3, page 15 of "Students Forum," in response to this accusation, M. Berezin points out that there are 340 students in the gymnasium and only 40 offices. There would be 10 students for each office and in order for everyone to occupy a position, it would have been necessary to switch offices once a month. That would lead to complete chaos. Berezin writes, "Please keep in mind that real talents rarely die off, but get to the surface despite numerous obstacles."

This is what the activity of "Self Help" looked like. These are all the nice and good things that it did for its members. Students' self-administration strove to make school life happy and to be remembered for one's entire life. Sadly, that did not happen. Hitler's murderers severed the lives of the majority of them at a very early stage.

The magazine "Students' Forum" made a very favorable impression on a famous Polish poet, Julian Tuwim, who sent the following note: "Thank you so much for sending to me your interesting and knowlegble magazine. I enjoyed it very much. Wishing you success. Julian Tuwim."

CHAPTER 4

THE LIFE OF THE STUDENTS AND THEIR DREAMS FOR THE FUTURE

What was life like in the class, what did students do in their free time, what were their interests and attitudes toward the school, the teachers, their classmates, their dreams and plans? Let's hear what they tell us:

Nicknames were very much in fashion at school. Someone who received a nickname could never count on being addressed by his own name again. He had to get used to it.

As for the problem of nicknames, the essay of L. Shtumachinowna ("Students' Forum," #3, p. 2): "An analysis of nicknames in the secondary school showed the following: cow, pig, monkey, sprat, dog. And the following ones are very much in use: elephant, *bocian* (stork), *kurczak* (chicken), partridge, *kogut* (cock). Nicknames are most frequently the result of the appearance and of certain traits of a person. Then "human" nicknames were in use, as in the following: philosopher, fat philosopher, valet, gentleman, mollycoddle, huckster.

"Those pupils who have received a nickname rebel sometimes, and you can get it, if you call names. For it rather hurts to be a "cow" for the whole secondary school, or to be a "pig," or a "walking post." But later, they get used to the nickname and have to accept it with a gloomy look or, on the contrary, with a gay grimace, because if such a pupil becomes indignant, it will not help him at all (then his kind colleagues will get on his nerves even more). That is why it is better to put up with it. Sometimes quite the opposite happens. A pupil can be eager to receive a nickname, but all in vain, because a nickname is sent to you by destiny. And destiny cannot be equally affectionate to everyone."

Lea Shtumachinowna

We can say we had a "guinea pig" in our class, and we also had a "*slim*" ("snail"), "little hare," "*kaczer-kwok*" (a drake named "kvok"), "giraffe," "*gele late*," "bogeyman," "*gele blintze*," "pine," "elephant," "donkey" and so on.

At the same time, a very talented pupil, V. Maizel, noted: "Every invention, every discovery, every new thought requires many experiments, probes, investigations and so on, and for that purpose, it is necessary to have so-called experimental rabbits. In the process of enlightment, the role of such rabbits must be played by the pupils themselves. And still, are we satisfied with our lyceum in the end? I believe yes — notwithstanding many things. Knowledge, actually speaking, is a difficult thing to comprehend, and you have to collect this knowledge first, then arrange and digest it, but we are still proud that we have the honor to do all that. We are proud that we are building the basis of the large structure of education, that our notes, works and experiments, our hectic searches, our preparations, and the sections we have organized, will be further used by the coming generations of pupils. We are proud that we cease being just machines that are drilling their homework without any thought, that we are investigators in miniature, discoverers, experimentalists, pioneers.

"What pride bursts our souls open when we see under the microscope preparations which are much better than those we have in our exercise books, that we can grow, and without any help, protozoa and hydra of our own production. Even an academic would not be ashamed of himself for such experiments.

"What a feeling of joy possesses us when we are able to make a conclusion by ourselves, when we are able to make a synthesis, and deduce a law out of innumerable works and books, out of volumes that are dusted over and out of scientific journals that had never even been touched by anyone.

"Our searching efforts in the reading halls turn into a kind of sport that carries us away and we are left to our own might. Both the process of growing something and the preparations lead us into the enormous hall of science, and teach us to make our first steps in it. And these first steps are difficult to make."

Latin had been taught to us in the lyceum of natural sciences and only now, when we were not studying it any more, did we begin to feel much respect towards it.

Now Chaia Shturmanovna shares the thoughts she had before graduating school. "I enter the classroom and the sound of well-known and merry voices meets me at the entrance. These pupils are dear and

Vova Maizel

Chaia Shturmanowna

very close to me, I spent so many years with them in the same classroom, on the same bench and with common books. Looking at them, I fully realize that the end of the school year is around the corner, and together with it comes parting, too.

"Each of us will choose his own way, and who knows whether we will see each other some day or not. [Unfortunately, the road turned out to be one of perishing for the majority of "Epsteiniaki." — V.R.].

"Leaving the school, each of us carries with them the impressions which they have had and which they have experienced within the walls of the school building.

"And this building that would invite us annually: will we become indifferent to the fact that it will never see us again? This building alone appeared to be a source for us, out of which we could get our knowledge. It has brought us up, forming our soul today. It was the only one that witnessed our misfortunes, it was the only one that was happy with us when it saw our satisfied faces.

"I am sure that the old building will nod its head noiselessly and will bless us, the youth, who are going out into the unknown road carrying with ourselves the stock of knowledge received here and being led by the directions and advice of those whom I am obliged to for all those years of education.

"I cast a glance into the distance, I want with all my heart and soul to see where my unknown road of life begins and where it will lead me. I am eager to know how exactly I have to set off, being uneasy, being afraid of something bad. I want to feel comforted, knowing that nothing bad is awaiting me. But I can see nothing. My glance, though strained, cannot in the least penetrate the curtain of the future. The wall is too thick and a glance cannot break through it. It is difficult, but I have to put up with it and wait patiently for the road of the future to open its gates of its own will. But to equip yourself for unknown obstacles, take my only weapons in your hand — this is the knowledge which I received within the old walls of the school."

This is how they evaluated their past and their future. They did believe that the most important thing for the future, the most important weapons to overcome the difficulties of life — was the knowledge that had been received within the walls of one's school. To think like that is natural, perhaps, for the majority of pupils graduating. But (and even to pronounce it seems frightful) all that did not apply to the pupils of the Epstein School and not to other Jewish pupils, who were like the Epstein ones. Quite a different destiny was prepared for them.

What the pupils felt during their classes . . . Let us give the floor to Hinda Drejzensztokowna: "A bench. A girl, my neighbor. My girl classmates are behind me, and my boy classmates are near me. In front of me is the podium and the professor. Thoughts, answers, bad marks. All that is associated with my place in the class. This seat is always the same when I am at school. It is firm, it is stubborn, it is exhausting, it is permeated with the mediocrity of everyday life. Outside the school, when looked at from a distance, it even has a specific content, which is filled with recollection: these are the pages the place where I sit. Mostly, it is an indifferent gaze, sometimes expressing a wish 'to catch you.' Sometimes it seems to be more cordial, promising future admonitions. And sometimes . . . oh, this is a real holiday! A spark of color falls down onto my gray place. This is a small particle of those 'sunny school days' that are spoken about so much by the elders and the authors. That is what you need. Sometimes the expression of this gaze shows care and sympathy, joy for your pupil"s satisfaction.

"And also, your seat in the class can tell much about your mode of living in a class. But what can you say about it, if you are feeling the reaction of others, that you are generally not in the right place? . . .

"Sometimes it can cause a feeling that differs greatly from the everyday lack of any wish and any dream to 'get out of this place.'"

These statements, belonging to a young girl, emanate pessimism, you can feel she is neither satisfied with herself nor with her classmates. But what to do? Not everything was always gay and joyful in school life.

This is how the first day after holidays, when pupils came back to school, was perceived by Miriam Maizelowna:

"Summer holidays have come. At last. Going out of the city. Hurry! The countryside! Having a rest. A ball, a boat, the beach, a forest, all before dinner. And after dinner: the park, going for a walk in the forest over the Neman, new acquaintances, friendship. And this is like moving in a circle. The days are flying by, quicker and quicker. The speed doubles. It is growing sad and more quiet. It is time to get back. There is a railway station at last, there is a train, a whistle of the locomotive. Saying goodbye. The summer has passed by so quickly. It must be so. Farewell. The train pushes off. After the summer, after the hot days, the fall days are coming. Then the wind, the cold. Books, school, labor, duties come after the holidays, and it is always so (this is the pace of life). Nice and fine things always have a tendency to quickly go away, but those which are unpleasant go on monotonously for a long time, it seems, endlessly.

Chaia Drejzensztokowna

Miriam Maizelowna

"The wind makes much noise. It rushes as if it's mad. It pulls at the leaves, the sand, small stones, the wind rushes ahead nonetheless. The wind has no obstacles in its path. The rain is falling down. This is the autumn drizzle. It is cold. The sky is gray, tin, the ground is becoming firm. Yellow leaves deprived of life are rustling over the ground. They were already dead when they fell down from the trees. A very strange atmosphere of fall is everywhere, the fall is triumphant. But what to do? . . .

"School studies begin with the fall. It is not so easy to get used to working hard now. It is difficult to fix your thoughts on something. The studies are monotonous, hanging heavy, like the ticking of the clock. Only one clock is ticking loudly, another — quietly, but both remain monotonous. For a short time, the clock may stop and wait for a spell. After some rest, the clocks begin to hammer away at the same tune. It is warm in the classroom, it is windy in the street, and the rain is pelting down. The teacher is instructing us, and the rain is looking into the glass window with great interest. It is pelting quietly. It is hinting something to the pupils. The wind also interested, pushes the rain aside, in a rude manner. The glass windows are trembling . . ."

The seventh grade. Helena Nemzerowna: "Graduating school, we enter the world as independent people and we do it with pleasure. How has the school equipped us for that? Has it prepared us for life in a proper way? Has it managed to give us more than a certain amount of knowledge on this subject or another one, knowledge that will be forgotten anyway?

"Yes, it has! Besides the purely theoretical knowledge, the school gave us a whole number of principles and practical directions. The school has formed our mentality so that we could orient ourselves to modern problems, we got acquainted with the culture of mankind, the school tried to instill in us the proper world outlook.

"Many splendid and joyful days have gone by within the walls of the school, days we will recall frequently in the future.

"The farewell to our school, to that carefree period of our life, now becomes a serious and even a bitter moment to me."

Pupils used to write poems. And how they did write! Rebeka Feinowna, an excellent pupil, wrote a wonderful poem, under the title: "To Live — Does Not Mean to Walk through Roses":

Helena Nemzerowna

Rebeka Feinowna

To live — does not mean to walk through roses only
And to dream an enchanted tale.
But to constantly go up the hill
And to weave happiness together with the pain.

•

It means to cry, being alone
And to laugh in public,
And first of all, to love something
And to devote your life to the something

•

To carry the unbearable pain in your heart
And to push away gray and sad days,
To water past happiness with your tears,
When the new one only starts to come into your dreams.

•

It means that it can be hard sometimes
And the moan breaks away from your chest,
Not to say that it is your swan song,
That it is the last sound of your life.

•

It means to constantly combat, to fight with your destiny.
To arise the ardour to fight in your own self
Not to avoid the hard blows,
To believe in the precious gift of life.

•

It means to proceed going ahead all the time,
There, towards the distant sun,
To deny yourself everything,
To make the dream of your happiness come true, by your future.

•

You have to learn to make the fabric with the golden frame,
Out of gray threads,
And to interlace into one beautiful scroll
All those strings that are trembling in your heart.

•

To live — does not mean to walk through roses
And to dream the enchanted tale.
But to go constantly up the hill, even when falling,
Suffering, loving — that's what it means — to live.

•

All that was written by the sixth-grade student when she was only fourteen years old. And she could also translate from French, Russian and Hebrew. Alfred Musset, Pushkin, Elisheva, Baudelaire, Heine, Pleshcheev, Goethe, Bialik, Lermontov — the list could be go on and on. All translations by this girl were, without any doubt, highly talented, if not more.

Perhaps she would have grown up to become a famous poet. But sadly, she perished at the hands of Nazis in the Vilna ghetto.

And how did they estimate their past in retrospect? What did they use to think about, how did they see their future, what did they dream of? We find answers to all these questions in pupils' essays, which refer to the last months before leaving school and entering the life of a grown-up. Look attentively into these faces, read the reminiscences about the life they led in the classroom, their thoughts about the future, and you will deeply perceive once more the atmosphere of life of that Jewish youth and the enormity of the tragedy that happened to them.

Listen to their reminiscences, beginning from the first and up to the last grade. Ida Galperowna speaks about the graduation from grade school into high school:

"Isn't it a dream? Is it possible that we are already the students of the secondary school? Perhaps it is possible, because a sign is on the door: High School. We have waited for this for a long time, and the moment has come, our childish dreams have come true. Professors in the upper grades will teach us now, and we are slightly afraid, but proud at the same time.

"We had a nice teacher, whom we loved very much. And she often made excursions with us to Zakret, to Karolinki. Our prom was the greatest event, we prepared various fancy dresses, and during class, we spoke only about the coming prom. No one could dance yet, so how could we think about dances? But it was pleasant to watch the seniors dancing, how they were dressed, etc. This is what we used to do during the prom."

Ber Charpak speculates about the various perspectives that the graduates could have had. "Sometimes, when I am just sitting by myself and thinking about what it all will be, about the perspective I have for the future, I see in my mind's eye pictures of life flickering, as in a film. These pictures are gloomy and dark. They are pushing each other and then rushing ahead, uncertain of the future. I am one of the senior schoolboys now and I am leaving school after several years. I have to make my first steps in life, to occupy some position in life, but

Ida Galperowna

Ber Charpak

how will this society accept me? What are my perspectives? Here is the first picture, floating right before my eyes. I used to be a cheerful schoolboy, and it was not so long ago that exuberant energy emanated from me. I used to be a good pupil, that is why I received a good 'maturity certificate' and turned over another page in my life.

"The new page has a gray background and many gray spots. He cannot continue his studies. The holidays are becoming shorter and he has to find something to be carried away with. Come to school daily to see this or that professor, ask him to give students for tutoring. They promise, but you have to idle much time away, doing nothing so far, he can start his own business or go to some businessman for an insignificant thirty zlotys a month, because this businessman needs someone to balance the accounts. At last he receives his students for tutoring, and every day he hurries to his pupil to hammer mathematical formulas or Latin words into his stupid head, all those things that could not help him in his own life, and all the work for ten zlotys per month.

"The picture disappears. Maybe, it is some special case and you do not have to be pessimistic. But to put out this ray of hope, another picture appears.

"He finishes secondary school and after many difficulties he has to overcome, he enters the university. He is full of hope and believes in his happy future, and every day he hurries to his lectures. He studies hard and is sometimes even cold and hungry. Examinations are coming. He is well-prepared, and he knows "for sure." It seems that the professor is a stern and strict person, but he is not afraid, he knows the subject wonderfully. But what about the results of the examinations? It turns out that he, who obviously was prepared so well, failed the exam, and his colleague who knows less, as is also obvious, passed the examination. Not losing hope, he decides to go on with his studies. He will graduate from the University and everything will become open to him. And he keeps on singing, "Gaudeamus igitur . . .," sometimes when he has butterflies in his empty stomach. He is in his third year of study. It seems to be the most difficult year of study. The next year comes, but he can not make himself attend lectures. He begins to look for a job and another of the unemployed appears. Pictures are changing one after the other. He has graduated from the university and received his diploma, he starts looking for a job, a lawyer tries to find a client, an engineer seeks to find some practice free of charge at a factory, a physician wants to work in a clinic. But who will give them a job? Maybe he will have to go on with the traditional life and become a merchant. But we get so bored of that, we have had enough of the dealers. That is why there is darkness everywhere, especially for us, for the studying youth; this is the situation of hopelessness. [I think he meant the studying Jewish youth in particular. - Y.R.]

"And the pictures are moving further. I suddenly wake up, it seems to me that I hear the sounds of loud accordions. It is somehow quite a different rhythm. These are the sounds of harmonic Hebrew words, which are combined with the strokes of picks. And what about the background? It is clear everywhere. The sun is at zenith. Here sturdy young fellows are working. I can hardly recognize them. It is him, my schoolmate, among them. How much he has changed: He is a man of slender build, the everlasting hump that used to press him down has disappeared, he has a tanned face, his muscular hands are holding a pick. And here is another one who looks like a German Jew. This is Teimonchik. All of them are joyful, all are working willingly. The rhythmical strokes can be heard, one-two, one-two. This is the thing that unifies them. Everything changes under these strokes.

"Here, the sound of an orange grove can already be heard. There is a large well of pure water that comes from underground. Down the plain among trees, houses are situated. And every evening, after the common supper, the melodical old Jewish songs can be heard, and your legs start to move and beat in time. This is a kibbutz that is dancing the hora.

"And he, my colleague, is dancing together with his brothers. He is full of joy, there are no troubles of how to get some bread, there is no fear of hunger that can come tomorrow.

"They are working hard not only for themselves. They are working hard for the country, for the whole nation: All of a sudden the film is interrupted. To go on writing or not to go on?"

In these reflections of a pupil of the seventh grade in high school, it is clear to see what was disturbing the upper grade students and how they viewed the real world around them. Unfortunately, their dreams were never fulfilled, because they became victims of the Holocaust.

The third grade. Ida Rozenberjanka: "A bell is heard. We are sitting and waiting, we are getting anxious. A stranger in a white suit comes in, he is a man of athletic build, he looks nice. He seems threatening at first sight (maybe only to me), but soon we make sure that it is not at all so. 'I am your new teacher, and we will have very strict discipline in this class,' are his first words. Laughter can be

Ida Rozenberjanka

heard in the class, who can think of the lecture now?

"A day in art class. A drawing class: thank God. *Pani Professorka* (a female professor) brought a red herring to class. She hung it over the blackboard and told us to make drawings, looking attentively at this live 'model' (yes, it was a herring, perhaps, but it was very bony). It is very hard to imagine, and, moreover, it is hard to describe how the class looked being so excited with such an experience. That is why we had a very enjoyable lesson.

"April Fools day. 'Prima Aprilis.' There is much excitement in the class. The students are absorbed in mischief, inventing different combinations from the sweat of their brow, the students get much pleasure, whereas the authorities are constantly distressed. Having no more imagination to arrange something interesting, we simply take to our heels after a lesson. We hide somewhere inside the staircases leading to the yard and to the room where the library is situated. We try to keep silent, and that is most difficult. Suddenly, the turning of keys informs us that we are locked in. Who could have done that? We are depressed. At the same time, we are embittered by the fact that someone could have had the nerve to play a dirty trick on us.

"After an hour of loneliness, we are released. Then we find out that Mr. Headmaster did it all. Angry and depressed, we have to go back to our classroom. This time, one of the teachers played a trick on the students."

All that the pupils had experienced during the whole period of their studies at the high school is very clearly expressed in the thoughts of an eighth-grade pupil, Susana Dyszkowna, who sees the class as a society in miniature. These are her thoughts: "Now, when I am already standing almost on the 'other side' [she means after graduation — Y.R.], when a jump into the future, into the great uncertainty, is ahead of me, how easy it is to realize what this class used to be, not only to me, during all these years, but to all of us, to those classmates, both girls and boys, whom we have been sitting with on school benches for so many years. Not knowing about it, we managed to create something bigger than simply obeying the dry timetable. Oh dear, if we spent five hours a day together, had so many common troubles, joys, aims, could it be any other way?

"And it had become a specific part of life, the world with a separate small society, filled with our own contents, the society in which everyone occupied a position that he deserved, where the initiative, the rhetorical abilities or the abilities to organize could find a wide field of activities and social activities as well. I can ask you now,

Susana Dyszkowna

what were they, those meetings of 'Self Help,' 'free suggestions,' voting, all those delegates, chairmen, if not the expression of our certain independence, of our social autonomy, all that could prove that we also had our convictions, aspirations, sympathies and even the struggles for position, for superiority, honor, that is, things which clearly characterize any society. And our 'statutes,' liberal rights — are they not the possibility to develop a society which is founded on the rights of a person within the limits of the state, a possibility which was presented to us by the school? So this time is not so very far away, the time when we were intensively working not on things we were obliged to do, but on things that could interest each of us or the things that the majority of our society was interested in. Being organized in these glorious circles, we took and put into operation the slogan, 'working on our self-education' (cultural or scientific self-education), and we also organized talks, the subject of which were less 'important, but more meaningful for us, more common for the class, about our defects, demands, and drawbacks: 'The Cream of Society,' 'An Undisciplined Pupil,' 'Individualities in the Class,' 'Mutual Relationships.' And walking to the cinema, to the theaters together, the warmest recollections of the impressions received earlier but now being discussed, talks about feelings, different opinions about an outstanding actor, about the stage manager's abilities, about the beauty of gowns, hair styles, and lastly about the scenery.

"Who can forget these excursions, organized in mutual cooperation, which enhanced our class life?

"But I feel I am getting sidetracked already, and my story is becoming more and more a sentimental melody with a sugary aftertaste, a tune about the past, which will never come back, but nonetheless still continues for us. Such was the life in this society, such was the free part of our life. Although, and unfortunately, you have to put up with the fact that every day which passes by shuts off another period of our school life, of our collegial community, into which we have invested desires and enthusiasm. Something is waiting for us, something in comparison with which all the troubles and difficulties of a student's life seem unimportant and fade away, but the joys of those days spent together will blossom!"

The sixth grade. Abram Gamarnik: "Being in the sixth grade, we have felt what it meant not to study, but to play truant. It is not the same at the secondary school, it seems. Who could think about studies and who could keep lessons on his mind? No day passed

Abram Gamarnik

without the absence of someone from among the pupils. Along with persistent truants, there also were the malicious ones, who did it on purpose, in order to show off; they used to go on excursions to Zakret Forest once a week or once a month.

"On spring days, Zakret Forest swarmed with pupils, not only from our school, other schools did not lag in this respect either. On cloudy, rainy days, when the grass was wet, we got together at somebody's place and had a good time.

"The results of our studies were deplorable because nine pupils, including eight boys, got left back."

This is what the pupils of the secondary school, who had already finished it, bequeathed to us. Let us give the floor to Paulina Levinowna:

"The chapter under the title 'Our Testament' is about finished, a new chapter is to begin, the name of which is 'The Unknown.' We are standing on the threshold of a new life. We have been dreaming until now. We are birds of altitude flying, we used to fly uphill, to float in space. Even now, it seems to us that the world is waiting for us, that it will stand open before us, if only we want it, that we will perform miracles, that we will make ourselves happy, and humanity as well. They are constantly saying around us that life is merciless, furious, that it breaks dreams and laughs at dreamers. We do not want to hear all that. Cares? We do not know what they are. Misfortunes? Yes, there are misfortunes. We lack nothing. Was there anyone from our environment who would not do anything to make us happy and glad, not to let the street penetrate into our angelic daily life? As children, we used to live in the world of tales as children: queens, princes, kind fortune tellers. There were two categories of people: good and bad. Good people were rewarded, evil ones were punished. Gradually, undivided justice, this world of fairy tales disappears, and we build a new one in its place. School and books have given us enough building materials. The self-sacrifice of the heroes, the love of your neighbor, nobleness. People who can grow away from the environment are neither good nor bad, but they are mighty, great. Which one of us never tried to discover these new worlds, never endeavoured to reach the remote light of a lighthouse — to accomplish a feat of valor. Years passed away. Mickiewicz. Slowacki. Zieromski. Orzeszkowa. Konopnicka. We wanted to suffer for the millions, to kindle the firewood of enlightment, to offer a helpful hand of fraternal friendship to everyone, to build the whole world out of glass houses, to love people. Their ideals — were ours, their heroes — were ours, and all of

Paulina Levinowna

a sudden, the anger comes, why are you still so young? And, at the same time, you are afraid that you will be late, that you cannot be on time.

"Life knocked on our doors. It opened itself out of the talk of older people (that everything was bad, that it was utterly difficult to live), it shouted from the pages of newspapers, gushed from the gutter in the streets. It said: Wings fail when you face reality. The leap from the dream to reality was far too large. People come down to Earth after they have been eagles in the heavens. Desperation and distress embrace you, and you lose heart. Desperation and the takeoff immediately after it: if we cannot find the world that we created in our dreams, then we will build it. And again — desperation. It is a pity to leave this world that has been created by us here, to leave it after one hundred days.

"That is why we are admonishing you now, our friends, who stay here after us, to learn to master this heritage. Take and possess our world, the fairy tale, where princesses and kind fortunetellers live. Our world, where selflessness, love, and nobleness are considered the most precious. This is our world, where the greatest, the best souls of people dominate.

"Take the heritage that is left after us, do not let this heritage perish; fill it with the love of your young, frank hearts and, what is more, with your young and fearless fire, and develop this heritage further."

In this connection, Joseph Gordon noted, "The examination for the diploma, which has been so widely discussed and dreamed about, is approaching in its solemn gown. This word, repeated so frequently, becomes a real thing. We will graduate the gymnasium in one hundred days. At the same time, we finish a certain period of our life and say goodbye to the school, to its joys and misfortunes, to its troubles.

"Let us leave the school years behind us; the years that older people believe to be the best, as do we. Looking into the future uneasily, even now we can appreciate the proper importance of the years we spent at school.

"We say goodbye to the irresponsibility, to the innocent enthusiasm, to the friendly and frank atmosphere and we enter the world fighting for our survival.

"I remember very well how I arrived in Vilna, so unfamiliar to me in those days, and the frequent tears shed during my lonely presence in this city. How many times did I ascertain with impatience that 'only forty-five days' separate me from returning home, and I wrote to my parents about it. Who could understand me then? Not one of my colleagues, not one of my teachers. At such moments, I loved to 'talk with a violin.' I used to play with so much pleasure, composing some pieces and giving them names like 'Nostalgia' or 'Fantasy.'

"My being late for classes after the holidays was accepted by the teachers as a lack of punctuality. Could I explain all that to them?

"Years went by, and the second period of my life at the gymnasium had come. I felt I was becoming more and more attached to the class and my colleagues.

"Today, when I am still in the whirlwind of school life, I speak about this life with pleasure. And how I will recall it after graduation!

"After finishing primary school, being free from the hard work of preparation for the exams, still being a child, I used to repeat the expression: 'Life is like lightning, because it is passing away very quickly.' This phrase, unfortunately, contains a great deal of truth, even more than enough: the school years flew by quickly, very quickly!

"After several months, I will bid farewell to my classmates. I will never have such frank friends in my life any more. Let us say goodbye to everything that used to bind us and I will go away from this place with a kind of fear in my heart. Where am I going?"

Malka Klauznerowna: "1932-1933 school year. The new year begins the same way as usual. Pupils are walking to and fro in the school yard or along the corridor. Meetings, shouts, stories, pupils are all interested who our class advisor will be. The new class advisor comes in. What does he teach? Nature and botany.

"During the school year, we create the 'Society of Enthusiasts.' In the winter, we grow plants in small pots. In the spring, we work in a school garden, we plant seeds and seedlings. How pleasant it was to enter a small garden during a break and to look at beautiful flowers.

"We realized that it was not only our work of art, but we could also boast about the fruit of our hard work, and sometimes we really were boastful. 'Have a look, this flower was planted by me, and these ones were watered by me.' It is quite understandable that we put special stress on the word 'I.'

"Excursions, what about them? Yes, but what to do if there is rain instead of good weather, or there is a melting period instead of frost? But once, the forecast of the pupils was not realized. The weather was splendid. We had a wonderful day during that excursion to Novaja Vileika."

The fourth grade. Liba Burmanowna: "I remember very well a great number of details concerning the life of the fourth grade. This was the first year that we studied Latin, and many memories are connected with the demonstration lesson. Latin class. Our classroom was located downstairs, but we were moved upstairs especially for that occasion. The Headmaster appeared dressed for a holiday, but his face was pale, as he had to face the several dozen Latin teachers. Everyone was trembling, especially when we saw the High Council, which consisted of people of different ages and different appearances. But we were lucky, so we left the hall as winners. Mr. Professor was the first to feel the triumph, but, but he certainly did not show it in the least. He behaved with a stoicism that deserves respect. An excursion that failed also comes to my mind. It was planned to be a sled excursion, but turned into a swim. We started off in the direction of Ponary Forest, but as it began raining on our way, we changed the direction and went to Zakret Forest. And returned back covered in mud all over."

Those were the days of excursions to Ponary Forest, to its picturesque places, and who could suppose at that time that soon this Ponary Forest would become a place of the greatest tragedy and annihilation, where the majority of Jews from Vilna are now buried, including almost all the students of our school.

The fifth grade. H. Aguzdowna: "Our life passed by without any extremes, without troubles and worrying, and what is more: in those days I desired to graduate from my secondary school as soon as possible and to enter the world. But now, when I think about the past that is so near and so far away at the same time, the past that has gone and will never come back, I see those days full of sun, full of life and joy. Only now do I see how dear they were to us, and how we were not able to appreciate them.

"And now, when the moment of graduation approaches, although the unknown future beckons me, I miss these years which I have spent at school. Wherever I am, I will always remember them and I will keep very pleasant recollections about them."

Berezin wrote: "I have realized that it is not correct that Latin is a dead language. This is the language that speaks to us by means of the brilliant prose of Cicero, by the wonderful rhyme of the songs of its poets, speaking the language of humanism and the Renaissance. The modern hall of science has been built on the Latin language. Copernicus and Newton expressed themselves in Latin. Latin was the language of Erasmus from Rotterdam, Latin was the language of St. Thomas Aquinas. Latin is alive, if the whole basis of mathematics and physics, astronomy and philosophy is founded on it, if every European has to use it, one way or another, even against his own will. But this is not the only question to discuss.

"There is the question of the principles of linguistics, about classical grammar, which is so logically constructed, and, first of all, we are speaking here about the characteristic features of the intelligentsia. The knowledge of Latin, of its poets and writers, its thinkers and philosophers, only creates the conditions under which it becomes possible to understand foreign literature. Latin is simple, stony, firm. But in this very simplicity of sentences, in this very primitiveness of its expressions, is its real beauty. Each address to a person sounds like poetry, vivid and subjective expressions of the speaker: the richness of words and the choice of these words enable one to shade feelings, to create a broad gamut of notions. And together with that, all Latin is extraordinarily logical. Latin is necessary in our education. School gives us a certain knowledge that serves us later, during our future life.

"Some pupils think that many details of education received at school, are superfluous — but such an approach cannot be correct. It is difficult for me to imagine a person belonging to the so-called intelligentsia, who would not know who Mendeleev is, or what the Continental blockade was like. Even a very small detail on the last page of an textbook is actually an important event. There, in the lyceum, I have been taught to master all the newly gained information, to take into account each detail which could seem to be insignificant.

"The knowledge of Latin keeps our brains working. In a word, Latin is necessary."

G. Rotkovichovna, a pupil of the secondary school:

"There is a silence inside the building of our school. There is no one in the school halls and in the corridors, and only a rustle from classrooms can reach our ears.

"Shrilly and sharply, and quite suddenly, the dead silence is broken by the resounding sound of the bell. The picture is changed in a moment. The gloomy mood of pupils disappears as if by the touch of some magic wand. The torpid silence disappears as well. Desks are banging, doors are cracking open and the pupils, like ants, are crawling into the corridor. They are pushing each other . . . A sudden wave is swimming in the direction of staircases that lead upwards. The keys in the hands of pupils on duty clank against the locks. This is the break in full swing. The school hall is filled with pupils in no time. Noise, movement, merriment. There is much running, laughter, noise here, there and everywhere . . . even the floor is creaking under the pressure of young feet, and long benches are creaking.

"Two girls are walking up the stony stairs. The first one is saying something interesting to the other one. She speaks with great animation. At first, her voice seems to tremble with worry, then the tone of it changes and fills with indignation. They do not in the least notice what is happening around them. They are both absorbed. The first one is listening, the second one is telling a story. They do not feel they are already in the hall, that a true symphony of human sounds is near them.

"It seems that the hall is one big mixture of voices, of heterogeneous sounds. The lighthearted turmoil is suddenly broken.

"A long and continuous whistle is suddenly heard. It seems everything becomes deadened because of horror, but only for a moment. And again, everything is the same old way. The same revelry, the same noise. Boisterous talks, lively conversations and loud roars of laughter, the symphony goes on.

"The careless hubbub is suddenly broken by the metallic voice of a bell. The clashing of keys and again a large wave of pupils swims down the staircases, down the long corridors and stops in the classrooms. The hall is getting emptier. The corridors are getting empty as well . . . The break is over, but not inside classrooms. The banging of reading desks is going on. And again, the crash of doors is heard. Loud repetition of lectures that were given for homework, talks, laughter. The second bell. The turmoil becomes weaker, the silence comes down. One more word . . . One more . . . The sounds die down as if everyone is expecting something to happen.

"The last echo of young voices bounces off the walls of the school building and dies away. The large school hall has become empty. The long corridors have become empty, too. Everything is quite. A sudden silence descends on the whole building as if it cannot place all these hundreds of young creatures, full of energy. The tramping of the heavy steps of the hall — a porter can only be heard from time to time. And again — the silence. And sometimes you can hear someone's muffled talk, and the silence again. A dead silence. Only a rustle comes from the closed classrooms" ("The School Symphony").

"The pupils excitedly discussed some serious problems of the school's education. And there was a change in the secondary school; a lyceum had been organized. The reaction of pupils was different. On the one hand, there was much criticism. The pupil R. Brantzowska: "The pupils expected something more serious than just the secondary school, that there would be no grades, that there would be no checking attendance, that there would be no 'I want to see your mother tomorrow,' they expected that the lyceum of natural sciences would do experiments, and the humanities lyceum would compose poems, that there would be a separate building and special uniforms, that there would be excursions, studies in the open air, and so on. All that did not come true."

Rebecca Belska: "The first grade — it is reminiscences already, things of the past, separated from us as if by a hundred thousand years. Now the work is in full swing, we are working like horses, but it is not enough, as it always seems.

"How far can my memory stretch? I can see the third desk right before my eyes, and a fragile and pale girl is sitting at this desk. She is permanently calm. She used to sit between two madcaps, she got so many punches from her neighbors that she simply could not move. But the teacher refused to change her place because the girl, she thought, had to work as a buffer between these naughty boys. You might have guessed that it was me — this girl."

The second grade. Aron Dvoretzky: "Joyful classes — they are moving like shadows in my memory. The singing. A happy song is literally jumping out of the young lungs to the accompaniment of a professor: 'One, two, three, four.' But the singing in the chorus caused many troubles. The boys tried to shout the girls down, the reaction of the teacher to the singing was furious.

"The preparation process for the traditional party appeared to be on the top of our list of joy. That was true paradise. And all because it became possible to free yourself from classes under that pretense. I was a 'painter' and an 'actor' at the same time, so I could make double use of that possibility. My role made me feel proud, and I prepared for the performance with enthusiasm. After the party, we got back to our hard work, thanks to which I managed to finish my studies after all."

A description of a trip to the countryside, thoughts, self-criticism — these are the things we find in the article "By the Campfire," written by Morgensternowna:

"At last, this moment had come. The evening was cold and dark. A huge pile of firewood was burning in a small clearing. The firewood was crackling joyfully, and golden shafts of sparks were shooting up the hill. We were sitting and singing . . .

"The latest events in the history of the days spent in the camp had all been entangled in our thoughts. At first there were all these shortcomings — the atmosphere which was far from friendly, the lack of understanding of the rules of mutual life and poor relationships among scouts. And then a question arose, must it all be like that? It is clear that it must not. And if not, what must life look like? How must we correct it? And, at last, what exactly is the essence and the cause of these shortcomings?

"We rose. A circle of strong shoulders had been created around the fire. Slowly, at first, and then quicker and quicker. We flew into a rage, somehow, quicker and quicker, till we started panting.

"We were dancing the hora. After the Young Scout parade, we were singing again, and looking at the dying campfire burning down with a wonderful sadness, which was not to be rationally explained. The second fire was like the first one. But once, when we held a discussion, someone declared that we wanted to have another fire, quite different, a fire that could mean more than dances and singing. A fire with a large and deep meaning and value. And again we were together. The night was cool. The stars were falling down, one by one. We were sitting together around a small fire. Only stars were twinkling above us and our flag was proudly hovering over our heads. We were comfortable somehow and we felt we were close to each other. We were somehow wonderfully fine. But all of a sudden, our Young Scout unit leader rose from his place. 'Today,' he said, 'we will have a trial for each of the scouts.'

"A name was uttered in the silence. Then the pledges were recited, one by one. He listened with strained attention and tried to memorize every detail carefully.

"The fog that surrounded us had at last dispersed. The day was breaking. The sun was rising. We got up, somewhat wiser, because we realized that our hearts contained something bad as well as good. And that means much, because once I posed a question of how to work in the scout organization? I was told, 'You should work on your own self.' And if you know your own drawbacks, it would be easier for you to work on yourself and avoid your 'minuses.' I was told, 'Take a mirror, wrinkle your forehead and look deep into yourself.'

This was written by a pupil of the fourth grade, Morgensternowna, in 1939. The author of this essay was an exceptionally beautiful girl. Little did she know that within a couple of years, she would be the victim of a brutal rape by the Nazis in front of her helpless and distressed father, our respected and admired teacher. Sadly, both of them perished.

CHAPTER 5

OUR CLASS (III B) AND THOSE WHO PERISHED

We are interested in that time when they were all still alive. The Holocaust was not to come for many years. But the memory keeps the fatal sign. The scene of the condemned, going towards the fatal ditch, sensing approaching death and demanding the world: "For what? Why does my life have to be cut short so pitilessly?"

I understand with all my heart that I do not have the right to let the memory die. Ilya Erenburg said very profoundly: "The eyes of the dead come to me in my dreams. They do not ask for help, for we cannot help them; they ask to be remembered."

Memory is related not only to what has happened afterwards, and to the tragedy that cut short the young lives, but also to the unrepeatable school years that prepared them for their future human experience. I would like to recall only those events from school life that influenced the formation of our souls and characters. They say, "We all grew out of childhood." Childhood and boyhood do not come back, but they continue to live in our memory for as long as we are alive.

So what was it like, my childhood and that of my classmates? The main focus of life was school and studies. The school united us inside its walls and, as they used to put it in the textbooks, gave us knowledge and connected us with the whole of civilization. In school, we were doing community work, conducting meetings, and organizing social events. We believed in the importance of what we were doing. That was the base upon which our dreams about the future flourished, an individual's preferences for one of the sciences or for the fine arts; there, our first loves and friendships were born.

When the young perish, it is not only their tragedy, it is not only a tragedy for their friends and relatives; it is also a tragedy for the whole world, since in every one of them "could have perished a Mozart" (Saint-Exupery).

There were many meaningless, unjustified military deaths in this war. Not to mention the fact that war and common sense are incompatible in the first place. But even so, those who went to fight believed in a goal that was worth dying for. My classmates were deprived even of that privilege.

My first recollection about our class as a whole is a very sunny one indeed. It is related to our tour around peaceful pre-war Poland. None of us could then have imagined that these moments could turn out to be the last happy and sunny ones for many of us. It was on the eve of the Second World War, and its atrocities and monstrous catastrophes could not have been predicted even by the most astute mind. Then, absolutely nothing could have upset our young souls. We were full of hope and of the sunny belief in happiness.

Here is a picture that was taken in June, 1938. We are on a tour going from Vilna to Zakopane, than to Warsaw, to Cracow and back to Vilna.

And here are fragments of the happy recollections of this event by my dear classmates. By the way, all texts here, as well as in all other places of this book, are from the originals, published in the school magazine "Student Forum."

Our Trip

As it was then described: (#11, page 11-13):

Rafes: "The Start. It all started at a class meeting, when someone proposed to organize a long-distance trip. The guy who proposed it did not himself believe that it would be possible to implement his plan. Nevertheless, this idea created excitement among us. Of course, when our teacher said that he considered it possible to organize such a trip, everyone cried out happily. The school principal also permitted a seven-day trip from May 31 to June 7, 1938.

"It was up to us to figure out the goal and the itinerary for the trip. We were delighted. Why were we sophomores allowed to organize such a trip? Our teacher told us that it was a first trip organized by such a young class in the school's history.

"Starting with that moment, you could see the movement along the whole 'front line.' Our teacher and the student-counselors whom we had elected were deciding on the trip's itinerary. They exchanged letters with campsites and visited "Orbis" daily ["Orbis" was a travel agency - Y.R.]. Mothers were coming to school very worried. Will their son or daughter fall out of a running train? Will the cable trolley fall?

Teachers and students from the eighth grade. 1932.

Our class on a trip in 1938 in Wieliczka.

Our classmates during the summer vacation. Vilna, 1939.

Our classmates during the summer vacation. Vilna, 1939.

Our classmates during the summer vacation. Vilna, 1939.

Our classmates during the summer vacation. Vilna, 1939.

The students themselves started to work hard on their grades. They were trying to improve their grades before the end of the semester because we had an agreement not to take on tour those who had a couple of "F"s on their report card.

"The group consisted of 27 people, including the teacher and Mrs. Goldman, who was to take care of our medical condition. According to the itinerary, we had to go from Vilna to Warsaw (two days), then to Cracow and Wieliczka (two days), to Zakopane (2 days) and then a day to come back. Finally, it was May 30, the day before departure, and all the tourists were extremely anxious. On that day at 5 p.m., there was a "dress rehearsal" scheduled (i.e., a check-up of all things packed in the knapsacks). The dress rehearsal went fine.

"And finally, the day of the tour. At 11 p.m., the whole waiting room for the first-class passengers was filled with the trip participants and, to an even greater extent, with their parents and numerous relatives, from an old grandma who could hardly stand on her own two feet to someone's little sister. Everyone wanted to say goodbye to the heroes who were going on a trip. Soon, however, everything was over, because the train started to move, taking us to the unknown. At 7 a.m., our train arrived at the East Warsaw station. We were in the capital, on the first stage of our tour."

Warsaw. L. Shapiro: "The first stage of our Zakopane tour was in Warsaw. We were allowed to spend two days there. We exhausted the program. After a sleepless night, at 7 o'clock in the morning, we went out to the Central Station. We were struck by the traffic noises of the big city, tramway bells, indescribable hubbub. We walked along Marszalkowska Street, Jerusalem Boulevard and came to 'Nowy Swiat,' where our campsite was located. The accommodations were not large, but nice and comfortable. We had not been assigned to any specific rooms yet, because another group was still there. After breakfast, we relaxed until 10 a.m. During this time, our instructor went to the city to order lunch. It is not as easy as it sounds. He had to order lunch according to the ritual since there are a few 'rabbis' (kosher students) among us. Finally, at 10:30 a.m., we leave the campsite.

"We chose to visit the King's Palace, 'Nowy Swiat' and 'Krakowskie Przedmiescie' first. On our way, we visit Stashis Palace and the Mickiewicz monument.

"A nice surprise was awaiting us. Because of an audience, there was no access for visitors to the palace. So we went back with a heavy heart. We went to the Museum of Industry and Technology instead.

This museum is considered to be the most interesting one in Poland. Salt and carbon mines in miniature are displayed in the first department. We would also see them in Wieliczka later. We saw all kinds of tools for agricultural labor, from ancient ones to modern ones. Then we looked at different types of machines.

"From there, we went to Lazenki by tram. This was our first trip on a tram. We could finally enjoy the beautiful park that was located by the palace. Sculptures of figures from Greek mythology stand along the long alleys that lead to the palace. Finally, we entered the palace. We left our cameras, put on huge shoes and entered the hall.

"We went from one hall to another admiring beautiful sculptures; paintings and portraits by the Italian masters impressed us even more. On our way back, we admired the original theater on the lake and the Chopin monument.

"Next to Lazenki court is Belveder. Since we still had some time left, we went there.

"An officer guided us. We visited Marshal Pilsudski's apartment. Nowadays, it has been converted into a museum. We visited the Marshal's private apartment, specifically the dining room and the study that was converted to a chapel. Here, we spent more time. Our guide saluted, and we stood nearby, serious and silent. In this way, we paid homage to the Marshal. In the next rooms were gifts and honors that he had received on different occasions.

"It was already late and we went to have lunch.

"It was somewhat difficult to get up from the table. Our feet hurt very much. Only then did we feel the fatigue. But in spite of it, we kept going on our way.

"We visited 'Stare Miasto' (Old City). Although this part of the city is right in the center, it contrasts greatly with the rest of Warsaw. The houses are colorful, the streets very narrow. The mood here is somewhat sad. This was at the end of the first day of our visit. Since we were very tired, we could hardly wait to get back to the camp, where we immediately went to bed and fell asleep. Almost no one ate dinner because everyone preferred to sleep.

"The second day started with a visit to the King's Palace. We liked the president's residence a lot. We walked through the halls. Every hall is more gorgeous that the previous one. Looking at the throne, we could not imagine that kings used to hold their meetings there. Then we visited the second department of the Museum of Industry and Technology on Tomka.

"Everything is there, isn't it? There are things from different fields of knowledge: aviation, inventions, the artificial production of silk and cotton, collections of chemical compounds. There is even a match factory. It is not life size, but is located behind a glass window and it looks funny; the guide pressed the button and at that very moment, the machines started working. In general, the museum impressed us greatly.

"After looking at all those 'miracles,' we went for a walk in Povisl. After lunch, we went to the zoo. That was the end of our visit to Warsaw.

"We took Marszalkowska Street to get to the train station. There were neon lights and bright advertisements everywhere. Half an hour later, the train was rushing us to Cracow."

Cracow-Wieliczka. Y. Vulfin and Y. Abelevitch:

"We left Warsaw full of impressions. It was late at night on the second of June. The next morning, we found ourselves at a modest but beautiful Cracow train station. First we went to the restaurant at the campsite.

"Everyone had fun looking at the Cracow cabmen wearing unusual hats. After a wholesome breakfast, we went on a city tour.

"Before lunch, we just had enough time to visit 'Jamu smoczu' (Dragon's Cave). Although it was difficult for some of us to walk the 272 steps up, no one complained.

"After lunch, we took a train to Wieliczka. We walked to the mine because all the elevators were busy and we would have had to wait a long time. After a one-hour visit, we went to the hall named after Sienkiewicz (150 meters below ground). There, most students wrote letters and dropped them in the mailbox.

"We were impressed by the chapel of St. King, made completely of salt. Full of impressions, we returned to the earth's surface. Mother Earth did not welcome us back. It was raining cats and dogs. Some time later, we returned to Cracow. Soon, we were sleeping like saints at our campsite.

"The next day, we started with a visit to Sukienice, where we went shopping. Then we went to Wawel, the oldest residence of Polish kings and princes. There, we saw many relics and tombs of kings and national heroes.

"We honored the remains of Jozef Pilsudski, the first Marshal of Poland.

"At the Wawel bell tower, we saw the famous bell 'Zigmund.' After Wawel, we walked, saw the Grunwald monument and historical Barbakon, and we visited many historic sights of Cracow. After lunch, we took our bags from the campsite and soon we had to wave goodbye to Cracow, the city of monuments. We went to the last city of our tour, to Zakopane, by train."

Deul. Zakopane. "At 6 p.m. on June 4, we arrived in Zakopane. The sky was covered with clouds and it was raining.

"We settled down at a comfortable campsite of the Association for Tourist Assistance. We had dinner there. We went to the city and our mood improved after we read the weather forecast. Our teacher made us go to bed because the next morning we had to get up very early to go to Kuznica, the first station of the cable car to 'Kasprowy Wierch' (Peak). Very early on the morning of June 5, we went to Kuznica. On our way, we met young mountaineers. They asked us details about Vilna. Finally, we got to our destination. A car arrived at the station and we boarded it nervously. During the twenty-minute ride, we enjoyed the unforgettable view of the Tatra Mountains. Our teacher explained to us with great expertise what we were seeing, specifically pointing out the mountain fields and the tops of the mountains. At the second station, we moved to the second car and it took us to "Kasprovi Verch". We left the beautiful station and many of us got sunburned. Many of us could not move easily after getting burned. Our attention was drawn to the skiers. Skiers in June!

"On our way back, we got really scared because at one point, the car was simply in free fall. At 2 p.m., we returned to Zakopane.

"After lunch, we went to the Stranicka Valley. On our way, we passed the famous ski jump in Krokwa. In the valley, we were fascinated by a waterfall ten meters high. We were very tired when we came back to the campsite.

"The next day, we visited the theater-museum named for the producer Khalubinsky. We saw plastic maps and fauna of the Tatras, houses of peasants, equipment and many other things. Then we bought traditional souvenirs. That was the first sign that our tour was coming to an end. At half past six, we were already in the train that was taking us back to Vilna."

Terrible pain and anguish does not let go of me when I look at the picture, or at the recollections of fourteen-year-old teenagers. There are twenty-five classmates in this photograph. Only four of them survived the war and ghetto (Vera Shapiruvna, Luba Kaganovitchovna, Nechama Baranowna, who died recently, and myself). Our teacher, Mr. Einliger, also survived the war.

Very significantly, class material characteristic of the the intellectual level of the students is provided by the short report of a court hearing performed by my classmates with students from the next class. It was a dramatization of the Robespierre case. The report was published in the March issue of "Student Forum" in 1939. Most of the fourteen-year-olds who participated in the hearing were cruelly murdered two or three years later, just for being Jewish.

Thirteen students participated in the hearing. Nine of them were from my class. Six of them were killed. Tadik Baziliyan was the chairman. Y. Belitska and S. Shelyubski from the other class and Niusia Kronikowna, Lily Mazur and M. Schwartz from my class were the judges. G. Shakhnovichovna from the other class and S. Deul and L. Shapiro from my class were the public prosecutors. Y. Merlis acted as Robespierre. G. Sedlis was his attorney. Y. Rafes and H. Sher were the court reporters.

The hearing was acted out in accordance with the rules of normal legal proceedings. The students made their speeches and decisions based on the facts and different opinions on the activity of Robespierre that they got from reading the literature. According to the six-and-a-half page description in the magazine, students used information from eighteen books on Robespierre's life, the French Revolution, the history of France, the history of the nineteenth century, general history, and biographies of famous people, all written by different authors.

The procedure of the hearing was as follows:

The court chairman, Tadek Baziliyan, read the indictment. It listed all of the major crimes of Robespierre, including arrests, repressions and the destruction of numerous members of different organizations and members of their families, of those who criticized the arrests and of those who did not denounce those who criticized. The vast majority of these were innocent people. The prosecutors (S. Deul, L. Shapiro, G. Shakhnovichuvna) also accused Robespierre that he "exaggerated the danger to his life trying to influence society in order to create an image of a martyr of the revolution."

After the questioning of the prisoner at the bar, the prosecutor, S. Deul, said the following: "The legal proceeding did not in any way refute the indictment."

The prisoner at the bar gave foggy and unclear answers and could not defend himself against any of the accusations.

Nor is it possible to see any extenuating circumstances because he strongly stood up for his crimes and so proved himself to be incorrigible which is worthy of the ultimate sentence." Considering this, the prosecutor demanded the most severe punishment for the prisoner, so that it could be an example for others and protect society from the vile influence of his personality. That was possible only under the condition of complete isolation from the rest of society because the criminal is not likely to correct his behavior.

Then the attorney G. Sedlis gave a speech. The attorney paid special attention to the fact that it was a historic hearing and that the person in question should be judged based not only on the negative aspects of his activity, but also on the services he rendered to France. He points out that it is necessary to answer the following question: "Who was Robespierre and whom are we judging? We know his merits very well. He planned and implemented numerous decrees that helped the people of France. He put the Committee of National Rescue at the highest level it ever reached. The next generations called him 'the Father of the Revolution' and 'incorruptible' because his only goal was the well-being of France and never his personal interests. He brought revolution to the culmination point. Suppose he did allow some violations. Can we penalize him for these small misdemeanors in comparison with his merits?"

The attorney submitted proofs that most acts of the prisoner were justified because he was defending himself and the Revolution:

"The French Revolution encountered social, political and industrial structures that were centuries old, and left behind itself institutions that were centuries ahead of time. It is also necessary to point out that the eighteenth century could not change because during this time, absolutism reigned in Europe and the peoples of other nations were not touched by the ideals and aspirations of freedom as during the "Peoples' Spring" of 1848. And in such hard conditions, there happened to be several people in French society who wanted to ruin this work through the death of the leader. Wasn't it right to punish these people severely and whip up the cases so as to persuade people not to do it in the future? Wasn't it right to create fear and a cult of the leaders of the Revolution among French people if the Revolution was so beneficial to the people of France?"

And further: "In conclusion, I ask you, the judges, to look conscientiously at the pages of history and to pass a just sentence."

The sentence

"On the one hand, we must underline his role during the most dangerous period of the Revolution, when France was surrounded by enemies like a fortress while signs of decay multiplied inside the county. Thanks to his willpower and uncompromising character, he took everything into his hands and therefore is responsible for all events; he led the fatherland out of chaos. On the other hand, it is impossible to deny that in the name of freedom and equality, he sometimes did it brutally, coldly, vilely, almost pedantically.

"However, because of his death, which he could have easily avoided if he had called on those Paris fractions that were still loyal to him to fight the Convention, now he is unreachable for the punishment."

In conclusion, he believes that he is accused unjustly, that he, Robespierre, is not guilty.

In response, the prosecutor pointed out that even if the attorney's proposition to consider Robespierre's merits is accepted, then we should ask why the prisoner did not consider Danton's merits during the case hearing. Then Robespierre (Yalik Merlis) himself gave a long speech.

He said: "I am not going to refute the actions incriminating me, but I will try to prove their necessity." Robespierre-Merlis pointed out that it was "a time when the existing situation started to create discontent in society, and that could have led to the triumph of our enemies. In this case, we should have been grateful, on the one hand, to the foreign agents who, being among our people, stimulated acts against the revolution; and on the other hand, to an unfortunate but absolutely normal situation in which the people of France were tired of the revolution. After five years of intensive labor, which resulted in political, social and industrial successes that no other country had achieved, after several centuries of labor there was a strong reaction in the form of complete indifference towards the slogans and achievements of the revolution!" And further: "If we realized the importance and greatness of the changes created by the revolution, we would have concluded that we should continue with what we were doing. So what if the country was tired and exhausted? So what if we can rarely detect energy and enthusiasm? It was necessary to continue our work, sacrificing even more people, since such great changes in the people of France, and later in all of Europe, are primarily due to it." The above described court proceedings clearly show the level of maturity, intelligence and sense of history by its student participants.

And at the Epstein–Szpeizer Gymnasium, I thought it was a regular class at a regular school. When I first entered the classroom, I was eight years old.

That was fifty years ago. I have forgotten many things since then. Nevertheless, one feeling persists when I recall the happy time of my adolescence and childhood. It is the limitless connection with that time, an anxious feeling of connection with my classmates, or as we used to say in Poland, with my colleagues. It is the precise and clear feeling that I am with them again, that I am back with my class, in the thick of things. But at the same time, I cannot help thinking about a terrifying and tragic difference. Half a century later, I am still alive, while they, almost all of them, are long dead.

I was attached to my class, I loved it so very much. And now, looking at the faces of my colleagues on the preserved photographs, I see more clearly the depth of the tragedy.

More that three-quarters of them were killed. They died suffering terribly, and many of them, as it became known, only after they had witnessed and survived the death of people who were dear to them. Even those who did manage to stay alive had to live through a lot of pain, suffering, tragedy and the loss of friends and relatives.

I will name all of the students who were in our class during this last year before the war, 1938-1939. I was unable to find any materials in the archives on only three of them. They are L. Shapiro, A. Berman, and A. Felerowna.

And now that you have a general impression of our class, let's meet each one separately. You will get to know some of us through an essay or a published article, the others through pictures and my short recollections. All of this are "short recollections" from the archives.

It is not important that some of the essays and articles by the students have mistakes, grammatical and stylistical errors (keep in mind that it was written by twelve- and thirteen-year-old kids). And my translation is probably poor, too.

That's not the point. Specifically because of the essays and photographs, they come alive not the way they were then.

This was my main goal. I wanted them to appear before readers the way they were.

Here they are.

Jakob Abeliowicz

Kubus, as we used to call him, was a good student, quiet, responsive. He sang the following song mixing Russian and Polish: "I have sweetness in my heart, like chocolate. My soul is pleased as if in paradise. A story happened to me, I'll tell you: I was sitting in the yard singing a song. Suddenly the mailman came and brought a telegram. Ah, Chaim, my dear, come for a rendezvous, at my address, Chaim Shmul, tailor. I went hunting, my face was torn and for a rendezvous, I'll never come again."

Jakob Abeliowicz

Funny, gentle, a modest and responsive friend. Why and what did you die for?

Henrik Bazyljan

"In the beginning of the school year, the professor told us that we should buy a book called 'Window to the World.' With great ardor, I started to read this interesting book. I especially liked the story 'Black Doctor.' The plot is as follows: trouble reigned among the residents of the Golden Shore. It led to a situation where kids had to be sent away from their homes to earn money. Among them was a small black boy, Deliman, who was at the head of a gang of boys that arrived at the port. They earned their living going from one house to another, playing the harmonica and performing magic.

"Once, it was a very hot day and they could not earn a penny. Looking for some bread, they came to the port, where they got a job carrying sacks with flour from the ship to the warehouse. At the end of the job, they got their money and Deliman returned home. For four days, he walked through the virgin forests. Then he saw what devastation the drought had caused.

"In his home village, an epidemic had started because of a lack of water, and people were dying like flies. Deliman immediately found his bearings in the situation and gave lime juice to the sick people. Despite the danger to his life, he returned to the city and called for help. The same day, the bus with medical help departed.

"Its arrival created a tremendous amount of happiness among the inhabitants, who were given water. The mayor of the city got interested in the heroic act of a small black boy and sent Deliman to London. He returned to the village with a doctor's diploma and became a defender of blacks. The hero of this story is characterized by courage, modesty and unselfishness.

"I especially like his fortitude. When his mother was trying to convince him to escape, he hurried to save his fellow blacks despite the danger to his own life.

"The heroic action was rewarded, because he was sent to London to study, and that is a big honor. After graduation, Deliman could have stayed there and lived without any problems. However, he returned to his home country to work for the benefit of his brothers" (exam essay).

Bazyljan was a good student, diligent, a very serious guy. He was always subdued, definitely very gifted.

Henrik Bazyljan

Mojzesz Bejlin

"I live on Adam Mickiewicz Street. I often take a walk around Vilna, my home city. When I go out of my house I see the red building of the Lithuanian hospital. I go farther and see Lukiszki place. As you know, it serves as a marketplace twice a week. The cathedral is not far from there. I leave the market place and see the modern building of the savings bank far away. I can already see the cathedral square and a cathedral and a basilica. There is a lot of traffic and noise on the streets. I can see the Castle Hill very well from the cathedral place. The Three Crosses monument is not far. I go to the top of the hill and the view is beautiful. I see many parks, gardens and cathedrals. Far away, I see the Rossa cemetery, where the heart of Marshal Jozef Pilsudski is buried. At the foot of the hill "Three Crosses," I can see the river Vilia. In a moment, I am peering into the Vilna ghetto. These are small, dirty streets. Soon, happily, I went home" (essay "A walk in Vilna").

As he wrote, he was looking at the dirty streets of the old Vilna ghetto, not imagining that in a few years, he would die there and that his relatives would die there too. His father was a well-known doctor's assistant. Bejlin had red hair, his nickname in class was *gele late* (yellow patch). But they were afraid to pick on him, he was very strong.

Hadasa Burstejnowna

"I do not think many countries can brag about their head of state as a person who did as much for the benefit of humanity as our President Ignacy Moscicki, because Mr. President, thanks to his deep knowledge, made several big discoveries and inventions. It was he who found the way to purify air and invented the formula for artificial fertilizer. Our President was born near Plock. He spent his childhood in Mezjanov. In 1912, he was appointed a professor at Lvov Polytechnic School. In 1925, he became a professor at the Warsaw Polytechnic School, and a year later was elected President. Since that time, he has occupied the highest position in Poland. The president's job is based on receiving honored guests from other countries, signing laws, going on trips around the country, and many other responsibilities.

"Poland may be proud that it is headed by a person whom the whole world respects and is grateful to for his beautiful and important inventions. And this year, that is to say in 1936, the decade of his presidency was celebrated with much festivity" (essay "I read about a nice person," about Polish President Moscicki).

Mojzesz Bejlin

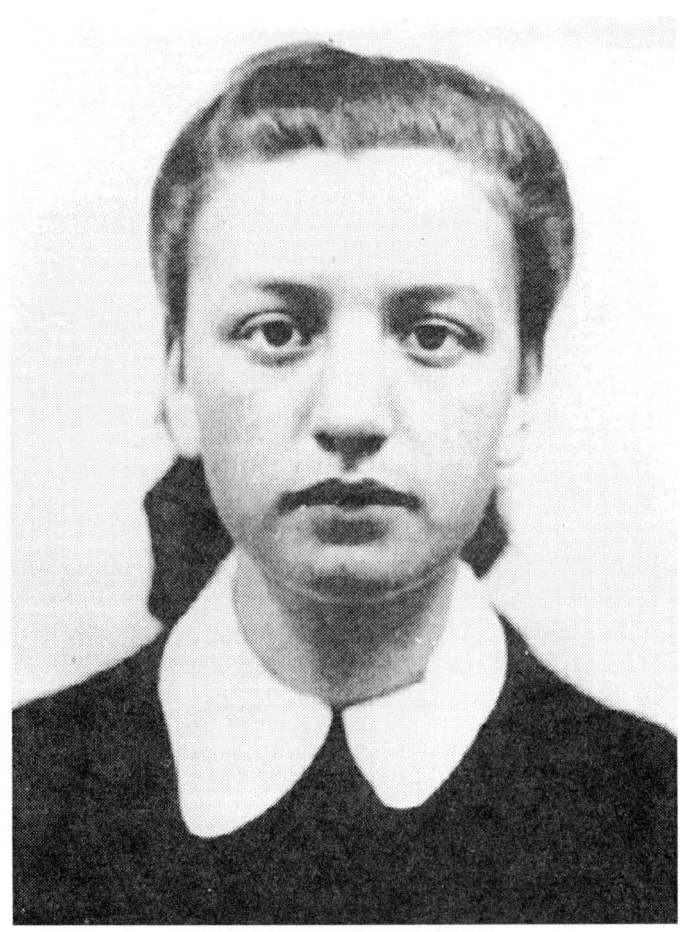

Hadasa Burstejnowna

Solomon Deul

Tall, dark and handsome. One of the best students in class. Always had the highest grades, only "A"s and "B"s. Very studious and quiet, a good writer, never got in trouble. Excellent in sports, especially skiing and skating. While incarcerated in the Vilna Ghetto, he fell in love and married one of our classmates, Sonia Goldman. They both perished during the Holocaust. Why?

Galina Danowska

Was a tall and strong young girl. An excellent volleyball player with a very powerful serve. No wonder everybody wanted her on their team. A good and devoted friend to have, with a sympathetic ear to listen to your problems. Perished during the typhoid epidemic in Vilna. One of the first victims.

Jakub Drewiacki

Drewiacki was an inquisitive guy, quiet, he liked books very much.
Here is his essay:

"Thomas Edison was a son of a poor merchant of second-hand merchandise. Thomas's father could not feed his family, that's why he arranged for his Tommy to work in the cafe at the train station, and a little bit later in the cargo car as a porter. There, Thomas showed his abilities.

"His first idea was moving baggage on wheels. Then he connected the clock with a bell and when the train stopped at the station, the bell started to ring. That was when Thomas, who was studying chemistry in the cargo car, knew that the train had arrived. Thomas also published a newspaper in the train. Somehow he became a telegraphist at the telegraph in Strefford. There he invented a device that pronounced the word "Strefford" every half hour. An attempt to connect two moving trains through the telegraph was not successful and the inventor Edison was fired from the telegraph agency. Tom fixed several complex machines for some businessmen and as a result, he gained their sympathy.

"When these businessmen found our about his abilities, they gave him a laboratory, where Thomas Edison invented the electrical bulb. This discovery was of great importance everywhere in the world. The smoking lamp that was harmful to the human body was replaced by an electric bulb. Very expensive gas lighting on the streets was replaced by electric lighting. On the day the genius and inventor died, electricity all around the world was shut down for two minutes. That

Solomon Deul

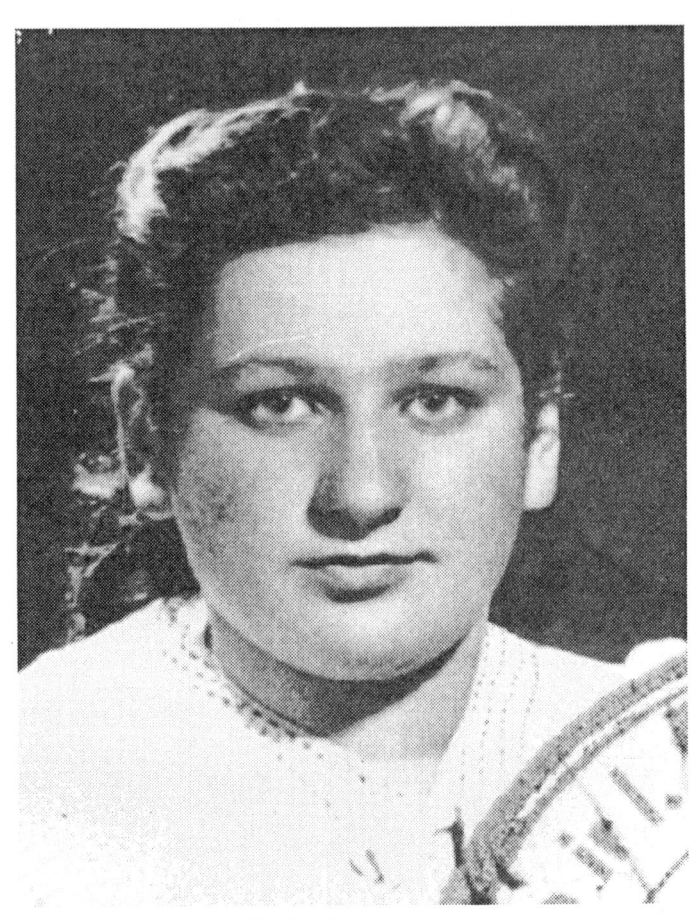

Galina Danowska

Jakob Drewiacki

way, they honored Thomas Edison" (essay "I read about a nice person"). He did not make it either. Why?

Maciek Gavendo

Maciek Gavendo lived by the Ostra Brama. A wonderful friend and comrade. A handsome guy, a very sociable guy. Loved to have a good time. When ever we were together there was always laughter and joy. Here is his essay:

"The writing of my first letter happened like this. Father had to go to Warsaw, Mother joined him. They had to depart that very night. After packing and right before departure, Mother gave me some money for small expenses and also an envelope, paper and a stamp, so that I could send her a letter. The next day, after I returned from school after lunch, I started to write a letter. I wrote a draft first, then I rewrote it. The content of the letter was as follows: I was asking them to come back soon and to bring me a present. I also wrote about what was going on in our house, what I did, where I was. After finishing the letter, I sealed it and asked my uncle to write the address. He agreed to do it. Then I myself put a stamp on the envelope and went to the nearest mailbox, where I dropped the letter in" (essay "My first letter").

Why did he die?

Sara Goldmanowna

A beautiful girl, tall, stately, everyone respected her, guys liked her.

Her father was a well-known doctor and assistant to the most outstanding doctor in Vilna, the famous Dr. Cemach Szabad. She had an older brother, a very good student. He escaped from the Nazis and is a physician in Moscow. She was a very good friend of Lily Mazur Margules. They used to spend a lot of time together, participated in many school activities and even wrote an article together, which was printed in the "Student Forum." During her incarceration in the Vilna Ghetto, she fell in love with her classmate Deul and they got married right there. Both perished.

Why? For what?

Here are her words:

"Poland takes first place among cultured countries. In science, it gave some of the greatest to the world, such as Copernicus, Marie Curie Sklodowska and others. Copernicus was the first to prove to the

Maciek Gawendo

Sara Goldmanowna

world that the earth revolves around the sun. It was a great discovery in astronomy. Marie Curie Sklodowska discovered radium, the rays of this element are used to treat cancer. Her biography is as follows: Maria Sklodowska's mother died. Her father was a physics and mathematics teacher. Maria inherited his aptitude for physics and math. After graduating from the University in Dorpat, Maria Sklodowska married a Frenchman, Pierre Curie. In a few years, Marie Curie Sklodowska discovered radium.

"We also consider Lukasewicz to be one of the well-known scientists. He invented the kerosene lamp and founded the first enterprise to process oil. Poland also gave to the world many famous composers, such as Chopin, Paderewski, Moniuszko and others. There were also remarkable artists in the arts. Vit-Stvosh created the famous Mariatski altar.

"Poland has great merits not only in the field of culture. Her sons were also remarkable, for they fought with great heroism for the freedom of other nations. They were Kosciuszko, Pulaski and Jan H. Sobeski. Kosciuszko and Pulaski fought for the independence of the United States. Sobeski defended Vienna against Turkish occupation, which is why Poland earned the name of 'Christian stronghold.' And so we can see that Poland takes active part in the progress of European and world culture" (essay "I read about a nice person").

Chaja Gordonowna

A lovely, outgoing, warm young girl. She had an older married sister, which was unusual for us. She liked to invite us to her home, where we used to have little dances and listened to her huge collection of records. Her parents had a school-supplies business on Zawalna Street, where we used to spend our allowances getting our own supplies. Lily Mazur Margules met her on the streets of the Vilna Ghetto in 1942. They had a long conversation remembering the "old" school days. Here is one of her essays.

"Thomas Edison worked for society. His parents were poor and despite their son's great abilities, they did not send him to school. When Thomas Edison was twelve years old, he was already working in a luggage car. He gave some of what he earned to his parents and the rest he used to buy books, because ever since his childhood, he had wanted to be able to study. He did different experiments and of course, he wanted to invent a new kind of light.

"Once, Edison saved the life of the station manager's son, who was playing very calmly on the railway tracks. Since that time, Thomas

Chaja Gordonowna

became a clerk and he had carte blanche for different inventions. Finally, in 1883, after many years of labor and diligent efforts, he invented an electric bulb.

"Since that time, Thomas Edison became famous as a great scientist and inventor who was of great use to humanity.

"Another scientist like him was Stefanson, who was also working for society. He created a train that was of great use for society" (essay "I read about a nice person"). Chaja perished. Why?

Herc Gotfryd

Gotfryd, nicknamed "Elephant," was a tall, handsome guy who lived in a building on Subocz. He did well at school. I remember we lived in a place called Lakhovichi, not far from Baranovichi in Byelorussia. He came to visit me in the summer and we went for a bike tour to the Svitez Lake by Novogrudok. It is a very beautiful lake surrounded by forests. Adam Mickiewicz wrote a beatuful poem about it. Our itinerary was like this: Lakhovichi-Baranovichi (25 kilometers) and Baranovichi-Svitez (30 kilometers). We planned to cover that distance in one day, but couldn't do it and had to spend a night on the road. We became very close friends then. He was a very subtle and sincere guy. Look at his open, kind and manly face.

Perished. For what? Why? Who will give an answer? Here are his own words:

"In a beautiful big garden, there was a pond. In the summertime, beautiful swans with long bent necks were swimming in it, and swallows cherished calm waters with their smooth chests. How magnificent it was, when clear, kind rays of the moon looked at it and made the surface of the pond silver. In deep waters in a charmed palace lived gorgeous crystal princesses. Some of them always looked into the skies; the others relaxed in the shade of trees and their eyes were green. They saw small Anuta returning home from school. The girl used to stop for a minute and give bread crumbs to swans and fish. The princesses loved her very much and every day swam on the swan's feathers to listen to her gentle voice when she invited fish for breakfast" (essay).

Rywka Himelfarbowna

She was a good student, serious, pensive, intelligent and a studious young girl. School meant a lot to her. She loved to read. She always had an open house and everybody was welcome. We spend many hours together just sitting around, discussing books and

Herc Gotfryd

dreaming about the future. Vera Shapiro Toper was a very good friend of hers. When she moved with her family to Warsaw, we all missed her. Upon returning to Vilna in 1939, she joined our class and we all looked up to this very sophisticated young lady.

Unfortunately, she did not survive.
Why?

Zlata Jozefowiczowna

A good looking, happy-go-lucky girl. She was an avid book reader. Was eager to share the stories she read with her classmates. A very close friend of Lily Mazur Margules. They were inseparable and spent a lot of time together. She and her family were killed by the Nazis. Once again, the question: why?

Ester Karklinska

"I came to Vilna from the provinces and immediately went for a walk. I had heard a lot about Vilna. It is an old city with many monuments. There have been a lot of tourist groups in Vilna lately who came to pay their last respects to the heart of the leader. My tour started on the main street of the city, that is to say on Mickiewicz Street. This street is large and covered with asphalt. All the main buildings are located there. There is a lot of noise and hustle there. Then I went to Wilenska, Niemiecka and Ostrobramska Streets. The Cathedral of St. Teresa and a chapel are located on Ostrobramska Street. Finally, I got to Rossa Cemetery. Here among the remnants of deceased soldiers is buried the heart of Marshal Pilsudski and the remains of his mother.

I also visited the Castle Hill, cathedral, the big university named for Stefan Batory, and the Jewish ghetto. In the ghetto, I saw small, dirty streets, the gates behind which Jews used to defend themselves. Finally, I got tired and I went to the garden where I took a rest on the bank of the Vilia river" (essay "A walk around Vilna").

Esterka walked on the streets of the former Jewish ghetto, not knowing that she would find herself in a real ghetto very soon and that she would die there. For what?

Ilija Kantorowicz

Ilyushka Kantorowicz was nicknamed "Piggy." He was short, plump, a kind and funny guy. We liked him. His nickname proves it. He was not a swine, but a "piggy." His father was a pharmacist who had a pharmacy in Antokol (it is still there). The pharmacy was located on

Rywka Himelfarbowna

Zlata Jozefowiczowna

Ester Karklinska

the first floor of a small two-story house, and the apartment of the pharmacist's family, where our "Piggy" lived, was on the second floor.

I remember how cheerfully he received us at his place when a whole bunch of us dropped by returning from our country ski tours. A kind and good guy. Perished. For what? Here is what he wrote:

"It was two years ago. As usual at the end of the school year, we went to a dacha (country cottage). The owner of our dacha had a daughter. From the very first day, we were friends with her. I loved them very much and they loved us, too. But most of all, we loved our ever-present friend, a dog called Burka.

"Every morning, our dog woke us up barking in the backyard. Wherever we went, our dog went with us, clearing the way ahead of us. It was the best dog for us in the whole world. But this happiness did not last for long.

"A rabid dog showed up in our area and it bit several dogs. When the police found out about it, they started to shoot down the dogs. When the news reached us, we hid our Burka in a barn. When the police entered the backyard, Burka felt that these were the people who wanted him to die and he started to bark. We were told to open the barn from which the barking was heard. The dog rushed out of it as if he were mad.

"There was shooting. Our Burka was killed. When we saw the dog lying on the ground, we started to cry. With pain in our hearts, we came back to the city. I know that we killed the dog, although not physically" (essay "Describe a memorable event in my life").

Niusia Kronikowna

She was a very pretty girl, an object of admiration probably for all the boys in our class. This picture doesn't do her justice. We all fell in love with her.

At parties, everyone wanted to dance with her, to be at her side, she was our first love, although a very childish love. She had a special power to attract; she saw that the guys chasing after her were glad when she paid attention to them. She enjoyed their attention but behaved very simply.

I remember her apartment on Makowa Street, the balcony on the third floor. We guys often walked there and did not dare to come in. We were timid. I remember the funeral of Nuska's father. He committed suicide because of financial difficulties, after the announcement of bankruptcy. I remember that the whole class was trying to give as much comfort as possible to Nuska in her grief.

Ilija Kantorowicz

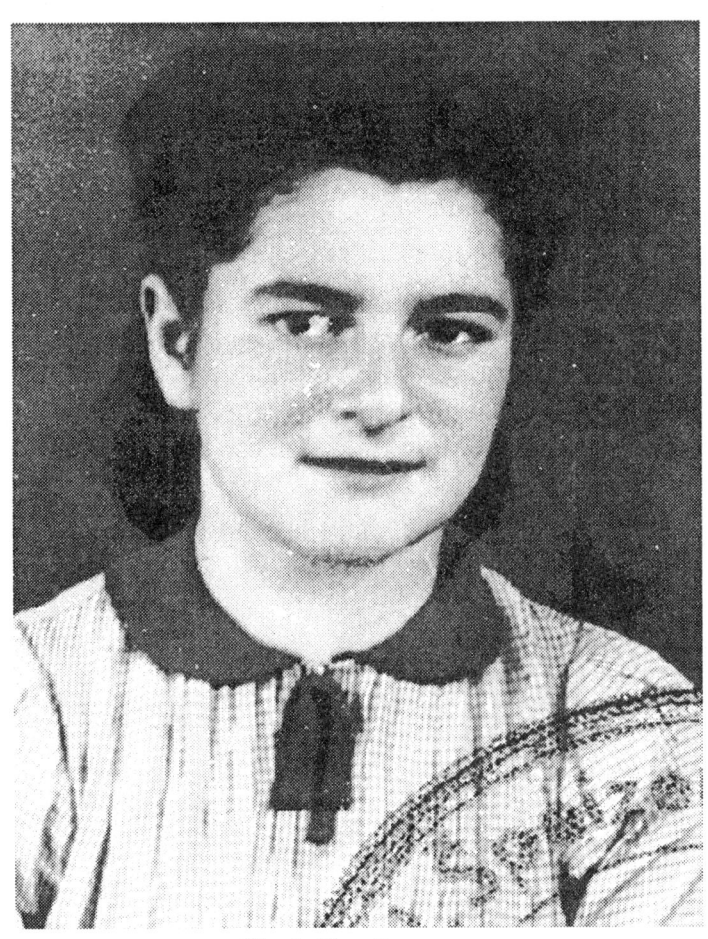

Niusia Kronikowna

Niusia did not survive, but perished, probably under horrible circumstances. Our classmate Borka Shub met her mother by chance in the forest. She was trying to get to a partisan group. Borka interrogated her (he had not met her before); she gave confusing answers, begged for help, asked to be accepted in the partisan troop and then took a handkerchief out of her bag and a picture fell out on the grass. That was a picture of Niusia. Her mother did not know where she was or what happened to her.

What happened to her was not unusual for Jews during the Nazi era, for she was murdered. Simply murdered.

Niusia Krywicka

A beautiful young girl, with long blond braided hair and striking blue eyes. Her are her words:

"It is turning gray. I am here and tremble because of the cold. In front of me is a dying fire. The earth is cold and unpleasant. If I only had a raincoat, but I left it in the tent. Someone stretched himself out on it and of course, I did not wake him up when I left to be on guard. If my friend had come back, it would have been merrier, but she went to pick up firewood. There is another fire not far from me, but it seems to me that it is far away. I am sleepy and in order not to fall asleep, I peer at what is distant.

"I recall that in less than an hour, I will have to put my backpack on and keep going on my way. An unpleasant feeling has overwhelmed me. Why am I sitting here in the cold? At home with my parents, I would have been sleeping comfortably. I would not have even dreamed about such difficult conditions. So why am I here? Why do I have to get up every day at 6 a.m., perform diverse duties, when I could be relaxing comfortably? Fatigue overwhelms me. It seems to me that I will not be able to do anything, but suddenly I brace myself.

"What am I thinking about? Do I have the right to think that at home it will be better than it is here? Is it because I am sleepy and I have no more energy left? That was just a moment of weakness and doubt — am I not happy in this camp? How weak I project myself. Is it right to be influenced by doubt? No, you have to conquer your fears.

"The camp is my second home, where I feel so wonderful and happy . . . Am I disappointed in my sweet family? Am I disappointed in the duties given to me? Every minute is not just very pleasant, but very happy indeed. You have to be strong and to control your emotions."

This article was taken from "Student Forum" no.19, p. 10.

Niusia Krywicka

That how Niusia Krywicka thought and felt when she was only fourteen years old, no different from any other fourteen-year-old girl. She perished only because she was Jewish. What an injustice.

Lily Mazur Margules remembers that during their walk to work at the Porubanek Airport from the Vilna Ghetto in 1942, when under Nazi occupation, her devoted Polish nanny used to approach the slowly marching column every day and throw pieces of bread and potatoes to her. Niusia perished during this horrible Nazi era.

Jakub Kuszkin

Jakub (Kukus) Kuszkin was a very modest guy, a good friend, we were friends with him. I remember that his father worked in the fur store as a salesman. They lived modestly. His brother studied medicine in Bologna, Italy. They always talked about him with admiration and pride. Kukus was a very honest comrade and a man of principle. Nothing describes his character and heroism better than this incident that happened during his incarceration in the Vilna Ghetto. He and his friend Boris Shub had to deliver guns and ammunition from the outside into the Ghetto. The risk was enormous. The penalty was death if caught. Kushin, who had lost his whole family, volunteered for the dangerous mission. "I will do it myself: if I am caught it is only me, you will bring death to your whole family, who are still alive." And he did it all alone.

He, too, was killed. I repeat: For what?

Feyga Melamedowna

A quiet, serious girl who kept to herself most of the time. Liked to spend a lot of time reading in the school library. Here is her essay:

"I read with great interest the books by Henrik Sienkiewicz. I prefer his trilogy to all other books. Some fragments from it I will never forget. The first unforgettable piece is the kidnaping of Helena Kurtsevichovna from Bar by Bogun. At that time, all of southern Poland was in the fire of war. Zagloba hid Helena in Bar. This poor and unhappy girl thought that at last she would have peace, but fortune decided differently. Bogun, who at some point fought with Cossacks, kept siege of Bar. After several unsuccessful attempts by the Poles, Bar was occupied and Bogun kidnaped Helena. In this chapter, I especially like the moment when Helena is taken to Dantsuvne. It was very quiet and only sometimes could she hear the howl of a hungry animal. Riders in the middle carried poor Helena. It is very scary, but

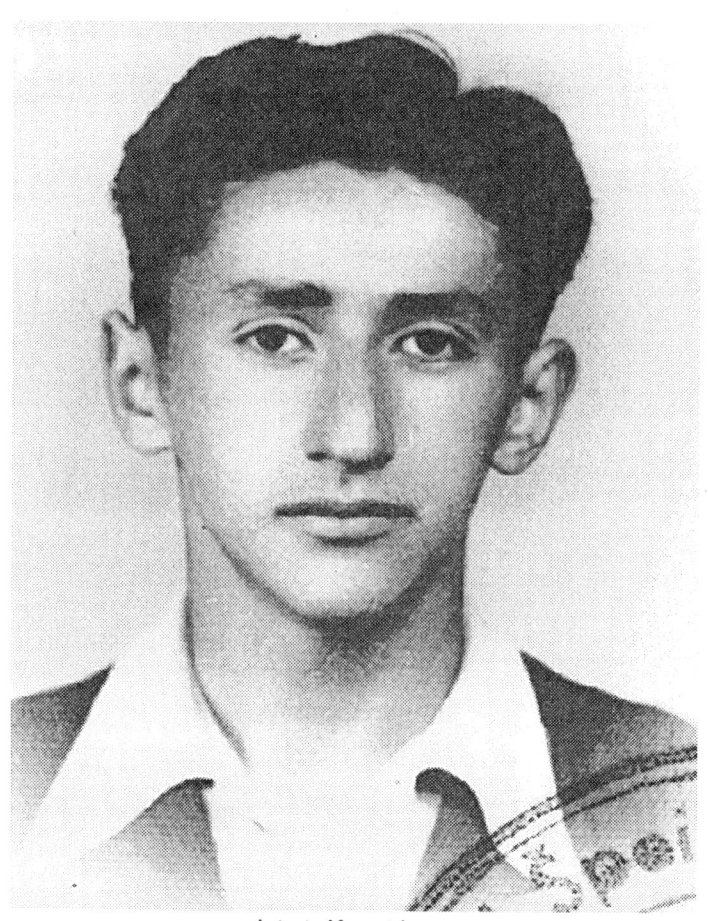

Jakub Kuszkin

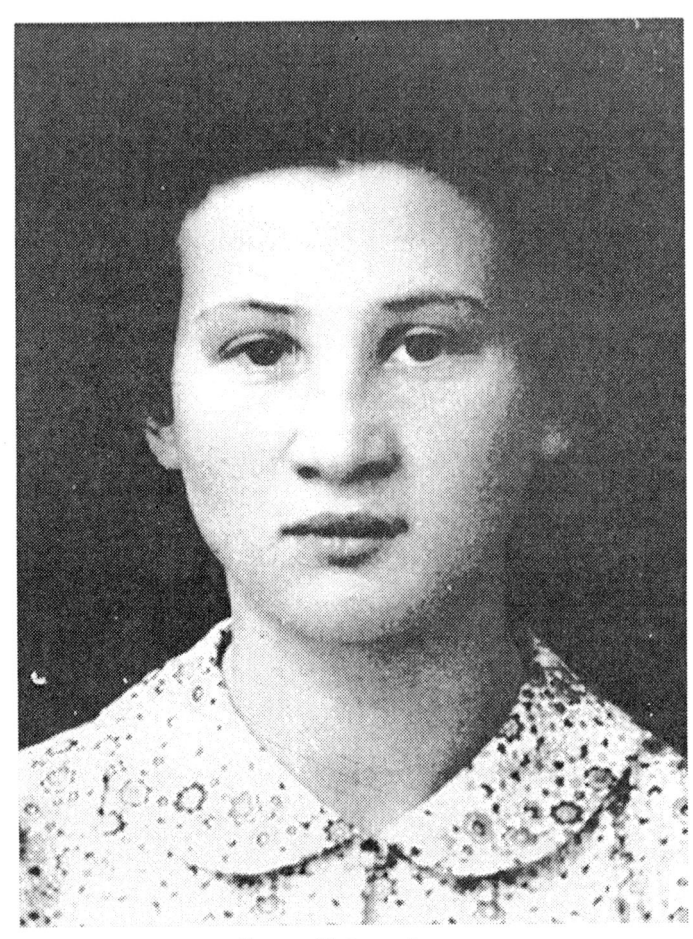

Feyga Melamedowna

the scene is described very vividly.

"Another unforgettable scene is the arrival of Skshetuski at the royal camp. Despite the dangerous route, despite the fact that Longi Podpenta had become a victim of this river crossing before Skshetuski, he was heading towards his goal to find food.

"Skshetuski was struggling forward on the bank of the lake. He had seaweed above him and water full of corpses below him. The sun did not warm him up during the day because he was covered with seaweed, and at night he was freezing on the shore. But worst of all was the lack of food. The moment when Skshetuski goes out of the water is very scary. All dirty and with his clothes ripped off, he reaches Maly Lug, where he finds several bones. After the meal, he keeps on going.

"In a couple of days, he shows up in the King's tent as a herald of the need and the heroism of the residents of Zbarja. Skshetuski does not ask for any honors. Immediate help to Zbarja would be the best honor for him" (essay "Fragments that I remember from the trilogy by Sienkiewicz"). Unfortunately, she lost her young life during the Holocaust.

Yalik Merlis

Yalik Merlis was a genius, I am not afraid to characterize him that way. From a half-century distant, that is the only way to characterize the unique abilities, talent and moral purity of this guy. He had only "A"s. That was very rare for the gymnasium in general and especially for our class. It is enough to read his speech during the Robespierre case hearing (he acted as Robespierre) to be persuaded he was and could have become a man of extraordinary abilities.

Boris Shub met him in Vilna at the beginning of the Nazi occupation. He looked terrible, was recuperating from typhus, did not know what to do or what would happen. Undoubtedly, he would have been a great scientist in the future. Probably another Einstein. And where is he? Over there, where the majority of the Jewish people of his age are, probably in Ponary forest. He did not have the right to live. He was a Jew.

Now, after fifty years, we still remember him with great fondness and admiration. It is a great loss for all humankind. We don't have his writing, only his report card, and that speaks for itself.

Jozef Rabinowicz

His nickname was "slim" because he was slim and tall. He sat at

Jakub Merlis

the same table with me. He had a remarkable ability that made him different from all other students. He could whistle with his nose. He did it really well. Often he would stand and answer a lesson, whistling. That drove the teachers crazy. They would usually ask me (I was the class president): "Rafes, what is going on, who is whistling in the classroom?" My answer never changed: "It's outside." But he did not use the whistling ability too often, that is probably why it remained a secret. He was a very cool guy. He never made it. Why?

Lila, Zalik and Marek Rudnicki

Zalik Rudnicki's nickname was "Rabbit" ("Zayats"). Zalik was my best friend. I was very fond of him. I loved him and to this day, I think about him quite often. We were also very close with Lilka, his sister (they were twins). Every time I visit Vilna, I go to the yard on Wielka Pohulanka Street (Besanavichus Street nowadays), go up the wing of the house they lived in, go up the stairs to the second floor and just stand there for a long time, remembering them with almost unreal serenity.

Zalik was a strong and very honest guy. He did not accept conformism, lies and bootlicking. He was a very loyal friend. And Lilka was almost always with us, we did not have any secrets from her. She was an outstanding girl and friend. I remember during a tour to the Warsaw zoo in 1938 (that is to say, more that half a century ago), we rode a small elephant with her. She sat in front of me, I was behind her and a photographer took a picture. Later, we often looked at the picture. Their cousin Marek Rudnicki (his nickname was "Mouse" Patsuk) was not tall, but he was a very good and gentle guy. He was like a triplet of the Rudnickis. Lilka was kind, strong and honest and had great respect among the girls in our class. Her brother Zalik and cousin Marek had the same kind of authority. And so what? All of them perished. Here is an essay by Zalik:

"Once, I received a letter from a colleague, who was asking me to write him more often. There were several stamps in the envelope for exchange. I did want to answer with a letter, but could not write it out. I rewrote it several times before I finally finished it with great effort. Then I bought a stamp and an envelope and sent the letter. In a few days I received another letter from the same friend and he asked why I had not written a letter to him. Then I remembered that I forgot to paste the stamp on the envelope and since then, I have not written letters. Although I received letters quite often, my friends stopped writing to me when they saw that I did not respond. They started to

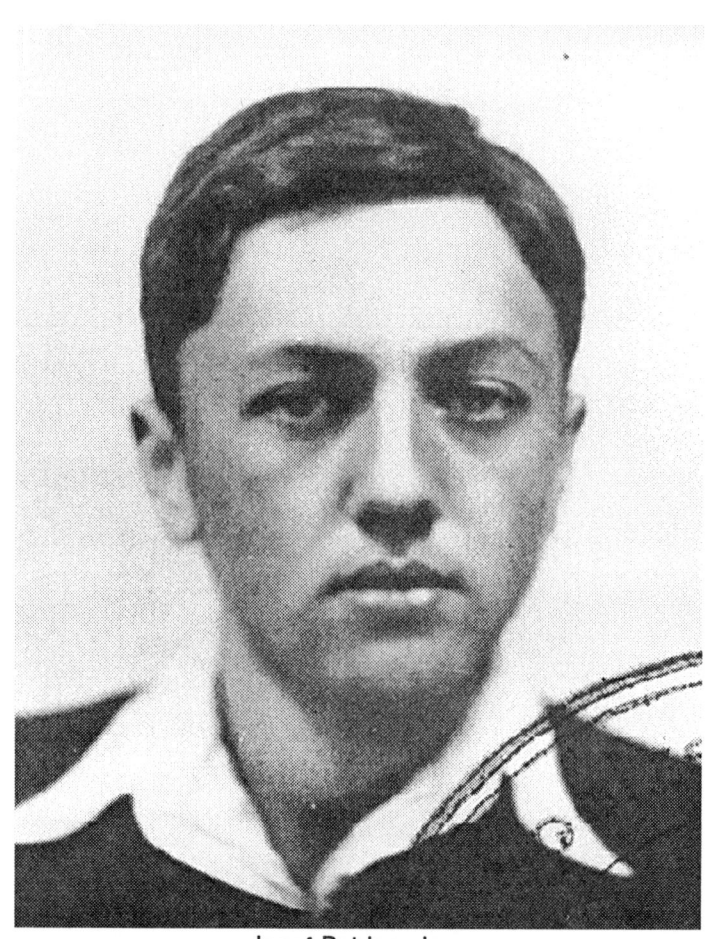

Josef Rabinowicz

Lila Rudnicka

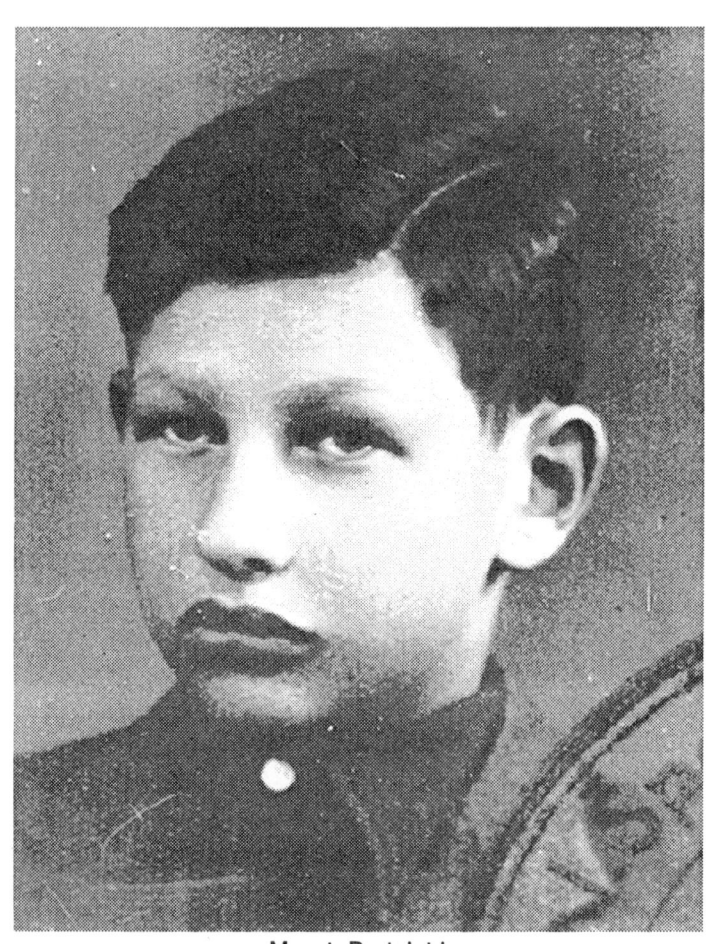

Marek Rudnicki

write more rarely and finally stopped writing altogether" (essay "My first letter").

Here is an essay by Lila Rudnicka:

ADVENTURE

"The job of a chimney sweep is very hard. Nowadays in the new buildings, sweepers just dip the whisk in the chimney and it cleans the flue. In the old houses, chimney sweeps had to go inside the flue and to clean as they went. Once the janitor and Yasek started to clean a flue. Yasek climbed into the flue and the janitor went to get lunch. He was not worried about Yasek because he knew that Yasek was a capable guy who could handle himself. However, Yasek got lost in one of the corridors and the falling soot covered him. When the janitor saw that Yasek had not come back, he started to look for someone who could save Yasek. Finally he found Phillip, who agreed to save the child. Phillip put the rope around himself and they lowered him into the flue. He was going down and stared into the black corridors of the flue. At the bottom, there was not enough air. Suddenly, he heard Yasek's voice. Deep down in the black corridor, he saw Yasek, who was pressed down with the weight. Phillip took Yasek in his hands and pulled the rope. In a minute, both were outside. That is how brave Phillip saved little Yasek, who got lost in the flue."

Izaak Rozental

A darling young fellow with a very pleasant face. One of our many classmates who perished during the Holocaust. Here is his essay:

"One of the famous American inventors was Thomas Edison. His father was a dealer in second-hand merchandise. Because of bad economic conditions, little Thomas was compelled to earn his own living. His father found him a job in the buffet at a railroad station, and later he became a porter in a luggage car. Thomas had many abilities, but he was mostly interested in physics and chemistry. He used to borrow books and read them in his spare time, although he had to stop reading at every station. He wanted to make his life easier and so he made himself a bell that would inform him that they were approaching a station.

"Once, when Thomas saved the station manager's son, the clerk found a position for him. There, Thomas figured out how to put two telegraph lines in one cable and he succeeded. Once a new factory owner saw Thomas's abilities, he asked him to fix some mechanism.

"Thomas Edison fixed it without putting too much efforts into it. Then he was hired at a factory as an engineer and there he created an

Izaak Rozental

electric bulb.

"His discovery made possible all of our everyday life and work. Now, we use electric bulbs, telegraph, and telephone.

"When the famous inventor died, lights all around the world were dimmed, and that meant that people gave him due honor and that humanity needs the invention of the electric bulb" (essay "I read about a nice person").

Moshe Rabinovich

He was a good, quiet guy who died of sepsis not long before the end of the war. He perished, just like many of our classmates. Here is his essay"

"'Quo Vadis' is a historical short story based on the history of persecution of Christians in Rome at the time of Nero. There are two opposite worlds here: the Christian world and the world of pagans. The tragedies are played out in the depths of human souls. Henrik Sienkiewicz describes the world of pagans very colorfully; there are a lot of descriptions in 'Quo Vadis.' I remember best the description of the fire in Rome and the death of Petronius. Nero started the fire in Rome. Nero wanted to cover his tracks of vandalism and so he pointed at Christians and said that Christians started the fire in Rome.

"Then the terrible suffering for Christians started. Christians were thrown to wild beasts alive or they were buried alive. There were so-called torchlight processions of Nero during which Christians were tied up to crosses, tar was poured over them and they were burned. After the fire in Rome, Nero condemned Petronius to death. Petronius sent the following friendly farewell speech to Nero: 'Murder but do not write poetry, poison but do not dance, burn but do not play the lyre.'

"After writing this farewell speech, Petronius organized a feast. During the feast, he cut his arteries and so he died. When he was dying, everyone knew that along with him, something beautiful was dying. But Nero did not humiliate helpless people for much longer. The soldiers demanded that Nero commit suicide or they would kill him. They gave a knife to Nero. Nero held the knife to his neck but everyone knew that because of fear, Nero would only prick himself and would never plunge the sharp tip into his neck. Then a slave pushed his hand and the knife struck his head. The eyes came out of their sockets and when soldiers granted him life, it was already too late.

"The last words of Nero were 'such an artist is dying.' When he died, everyone knew that along with him everything bad died. So Nero blew over like a storm, a wind or pestilence" (essay "The chapters from 'Quo Vadis' that I remembered the best").

Henoch Sosenski

Sosenski, whose nickname was "Sosna" ("pine tree"), was a quiet and calm guy and never participated in our class tricks. He perished during the Nazi era.

"Edison was a big inventor. We spend many winter evenings under an electric bulb and we owe it to him. When he was young, Edison sold newspapers at the train station. Because his father was poor and could not find any job for his son except selling newspapers, he used to study in a luggage car. Whenever he had a free minute, he borrowed books at the library in Detroit. The conductor did not approve of his reading, he said that Edison was just wasting time.

"With the money he earned, he bought a small 'laboratory' that consisted of several bottles with different chemicals. Darkness did not allow Edison to read books. That is why he decided to invent a new lighting system.

"Once, during his experiments, a fire started on the floor and the furious conductor threw his laboratory under the train. Once, Edison was waiting for an approaching train and he saw that a child was playing on the railroad tracks. Edison saved the child. It turned out that it was the child of the station manager. As an reward for this, he taught Edison how to handle the telegraph machine and later, after much trouble, he obtained a job at the telegraph agency. After several years of work, he invented an electric bulb that we still use.

"He is the greatest contemporary inventor. Had Edison not exploited electricity, we would not have had many devices that are operated by electricity.

"When Edison died, all electrical stations all around the world turned the electricity off to show the great inventor that the whole world was mourning" (essay "I read about a nice person").

Rosa Szejnermanowna

She was a quiet and shy little girl. An only daughter, she was pampered by her loving parents. She did not socialize much with us, mostly staying in the company of her mother. She died during the Nazi Era. Here is her essay:

"The job of chimney sweep is very dangerous. A guy named Yas was a chimney sweep. That is why he went to clean the chimney with an old chimney sweep. The old chimney sweep left Yas alone for a second, but he was not careful and got stuck inside the chimney. When

Henoch Sosenski

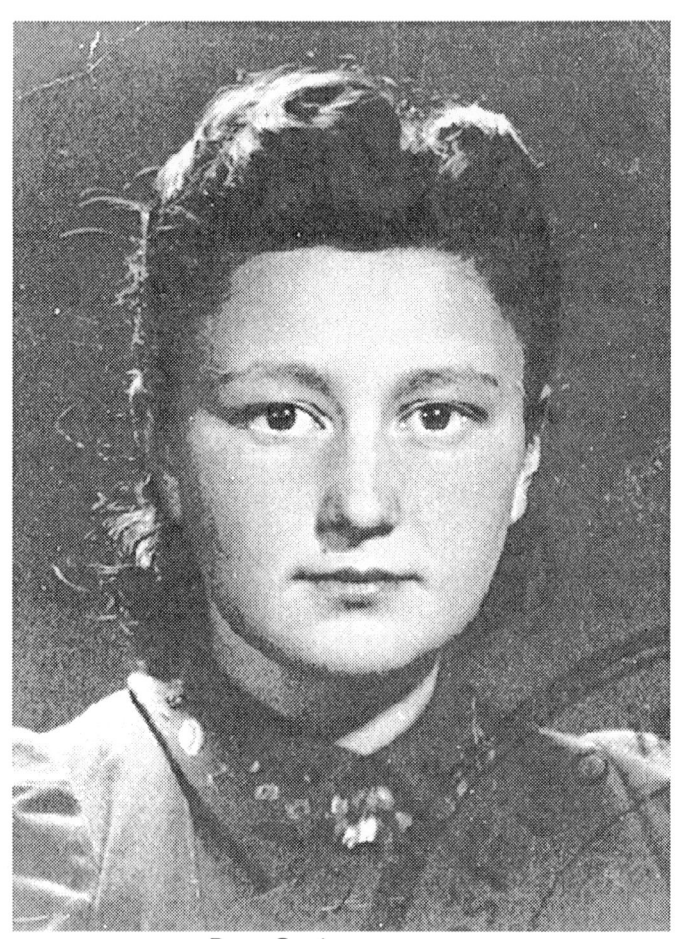

Rosa Szejnermanowna

the chimney sweep came back, Yas was not there. Very upset, he ran into the street. A lot of people were standing on the street and looking at the chimney, but no one was brave enough to save the boy. Suddenly one gentleman from the crowd climbed to the chimney. It was Phillip, the boy's guardian. There was a lot of smoke, spider webs and soot on the way. After a lot of work, Phillip found Yas, told him to climb on his shoulders and together they got out of the chimney" (essay "Adventures of a chimney sweep").

Chaim Sher

Here is one of his school essays:

"Our house is located on Rudnicka Street. It has a pit and one floor. Great noise reigns here because it is the city center. Cars, carts and horse-driven cabs move there all the time. The backyard is small and so we cannot play there.

"In the middle of the backyard, there is a round court surrounded by wire. We occupy apartment #1, Mrs. G. occupies apartment #2 and apartment #3 is available.

"Across the way lives the owner, who occupies a large apartment. In the pit, there is a store. In the backyard lives a woman with a big dog.

"This dog barks a long time and with passion. There is a sugar storage in the pit. On the storage wall there is a sign: 'Sugar makes us stronger.' There is also a bag storage and guard's apartment in the pit. The guard's dog is meek and seldom barks. Our apartment has four rooms and a kitchen. There are three windows looking out at the backyard in our apartment and five windows looking out on Rudnicka Street. The backyard is paved" (essay "Our house and its residents"). He perished. Why?

Mark Schwarc

One of our classmates who never had a chance. He lost his young life during the Holocaust. Here is his essay:

"Voyages to the Poles of the Earth had a practical goal, the discovery of a path to Japan through the Arctic Ocean and the use of minerals, and also a scientific goal, the discovery of new countries. There was also a story about the northwest route that was discovered by Mak Kler when he was searching for the Franklin expedition that had disappeared. However, Mak Kler did not manage to travel the route. Fritief Nansen from Norway and Romuald Amundsen especially proved themselves during expeditions to the poles. On board the ship

Chaim Scher

Mark Schwarc

"From," Amundsen was heading towards the North Pole, but at that same time, Peary had already reached it. On the other hand, Amundsen wanted somehow to compensate for the lack of luck and so he turned toward the South Pole. Because of damage, the ship "From" was sent away. Amundsen and two of his friends loaded a plane with dogs and sleds, took some food and flew to Antarctica. After several days of flying, the plane crashed. People, sleds and dogs saved themselves. The temperature was -40 C, but they put up tents and waited until the temperature rose. When the temperature reached -20 C, they started on their way on the sleds. They reached the South Pole, which they called 'Plateau Gakovno,' and went back.

"On the way back, they met a ship and returned to Norway.

"After the World War, Amundsen bought two airplanes, H24 and H25, and flew to study the North Pole region. He flew over the northwest route that he was the first to discover and he was to land one degree away from the Pole. During the landing, the plane crashed. He had just enough gas to come back to Spitsbergen. In Spitsbergen, he was met by a Norwegian torpedo boat and an squadron plane. Amundsen died while they were looking for Nobile (essay "I read about a nice person").

Jakob Steinberg

A tall and handsome fellow. Very good mathematically, and there are two examples of a math test he took and solved with flying colors. Perished at the hands of the SS. Why?

Math examination:

1. A merchant mixed 14 kilograms of coffee priced at 16.5 zlotys per kilo and 16 kilograms of coffee priced at 3/4 zlotys per kilo.

Find out the net price for the mix per kilo. Find out the selling price per kilo of the mix if the merchant's mark-up was 20%.

2. A rectangular territory with sides of 33.5 and 23.7 meters is surrounded with a fence. What was the total cost for the fence if one meter of it costs 7.9 zlotys?

Answers: 1. The merchant was selling for 21.24 zlotys per kilo. 2. The whole fence cost 813 zlotys.

Jakob Wulfin

He was an exceptionally good-looking guy. Girls used to fall all over him, but at that time he was more interested in sports and school. He loved to ski and skate. In the spring, summer and fall we used to go bicycling out of town. Here are his own words:

Jakob Steinberg

Jakob Wulfin

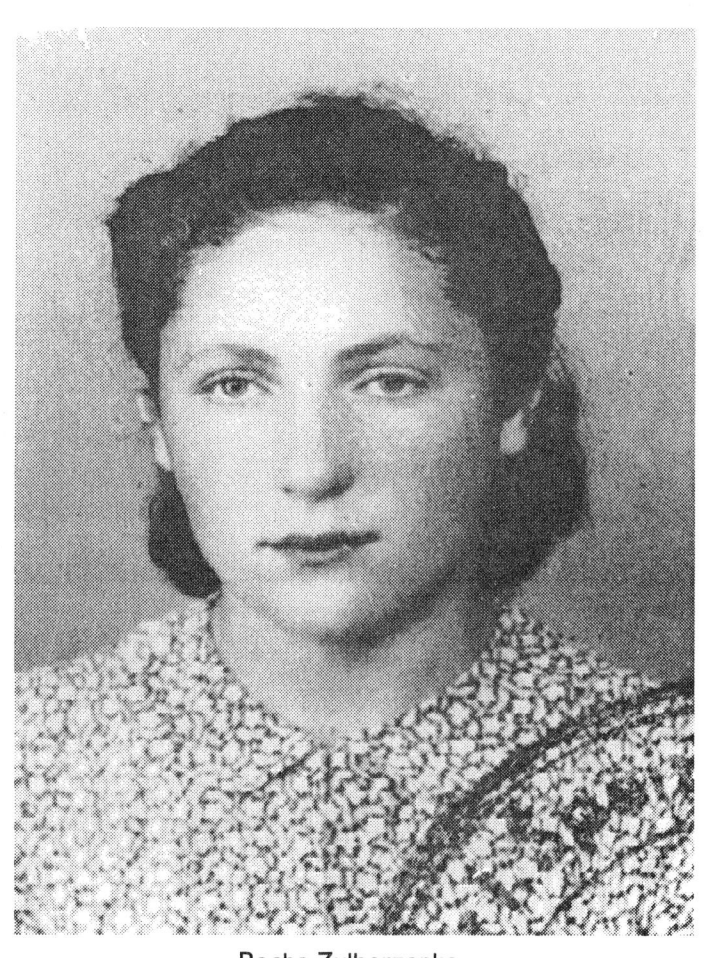

Rocha Zylberzanka

""When I had just mastered reading skills, I decided to write a letter. I saw many times that adults send and receive mail and I also wanted to do it. But I did not have anybody to write a letter to. Only in the summer did I have an occasion. We went to the country and suddenly, because of some important trading business, my father had to go to the city. My mother wrote him a letter and then I wanted to write something, too. I took a piece of paper, a pen and started to write. It was very difficult at first and I was just scribbling, but later I started to write rather well. It was a short letter, it only contained a request to bring me a gift and I was just saying hi, but from my point of view it was already a masterpiece. I put it in the envelope very solemnly, put a stamp on it and dropped it in the mailbox. It was like performing a ceremony then and now, since I write letters quite often, it seems to me very funny" (essay "My first letter").

He never had a chance. Why?

Rocha Zylberzanka

An attractive, tall, red-headed girl with freckles on her quiet pretty face. She was a very close friend of Luba Kaganowicz. They were inseparable, always sitting or walking side by side. She never had a chance. Here are her words:

"Vilna is an old city with a lot of monuments and cathedrals with a rich history. I spent most of my childhood in Warsaw. I was very attracted to Vilna and dreamed to visit it at least once. My dreams became a reality once I came to Vilna. The first place that I visited was the Rossa Cemetery, where the mausoleum was located. I also visited the cathedral and many tombs of Polish kings. This city is full of noise and movement. The cars, bicycles and cabs rush on the streets. The biggest street in Vilna is Mickiewicz Street.

There is the Stefan Batory University in Vilna, many different buildings and Narocz Lake, well-known all around Poland. I left Vilna, but I am sure to come back soon" (essay "A walk around Vilna").

CHAPTER 6

THOSE WHO SURVIVED FIFTY YEARS LATER

Dodz'ka Kremer

Doksa, as we called him, was a good guy, a little on a heavy side, he used to live on the Bufalovs Mountain Street that was right in the center of the city. Everyone in the class loved him.

We can clearly understand what his interests and aspirations were from his school composition. Let us read what he wrote in his essay: "Inventions and discoveries are of the utmost, even colossal, importance. That is why people are constantly working in order to enrich themselves and mankind by their inventions and discoveries. The Frenchman, Pasteur, was one of the most famous inventors. He invented the vaccine that has already saved thousands of children's lives and grown-up people that were horribly bitten by mad dogs. Mankind can be grateful to many other people too." And here, Dodz'ka recalls Edison, Stevenson, Gutenberg, Sklodowska-Curie. He wrote: "One hundred years have passed since the first railroad was built, but look at how much the appearance of all civilized states has changed. It happens sometimes that even a very small invention can cause big changes. Let us take for instance, the invention of printing. Jan Gutenberg invented printing. And this invention was of great importance. We would have never had our modern newspaper, or a book, or school press without this invention.

"However, a human mind can never stop working. There are even people who devote their whole life to some idea the same way as Curie did" (school composition "I read about a nice person").

Nehama Baranowna

I remember this girl very well. She was serious and independent. She did well, and she was especially good at mathematics and physics.

Nehama Baranowna

She survived and emigrated to America. There she became a professor of economics and taught at Boston University. She died quite recently.

A tall, strong girl who liked sports and was very good at it. In school, she was very popular and everyone wanted her on their team. Vera Toper met her after the war in New York. She was a sophisticated young lady with many plans for the future. She loved music and I remember going with her to Carnegie Hall to listen to the not yet famous Pavarotti.

Rachela Kownerowna (nee Kozlowski)

In September of 1995, Rachel Kozlowski came to New York on a visit from London. It was a very happy occasion. After almost fifty years, the schoolmates of the Epstein–Szpeizer Gymnasium got together. There were six of us from the same class: Abrasha Santocki, Yulian Rafes, Gabik Sedlis, Lily Mazurowna-Margules, Rachel Kozlovski and Vera Shapirowna-Toper. There was a lot of reminiscence and nostalgia.

Here is Rachel's story:

Her father was killed by the Nazis right at the beginning of the war. Her mother and the rest of the family was separated from Rachel, they were taken to prison and consequently killed. Here was Rachel, a young innocent girl, trying to fend for herself. She was lucky to find her aunt, who took care of her. Life in the ghetto was hard and dangerous. One never knew what was in store for them. Rachel spent two years there, from '41 to '43. Her uncle found out that the ghetto would be liquidated and the Jews taken to different camps and many would be killed. Her uncle had a Polish friend who lived on the outskirts of Vilna. She allowed him to build a bunker on her property, where twenty people hid from the Nazi. The Polish lady supplied them with food, for which they paid, and they spent almost a year there.

In the meantime, the Russians were coming closer to Vilna and the front was established right where their bunker was. The fighting was very intense and they were constantly in danger until they were liberated by the Russians. After the liberation, life was not much easier. They knew they had to leave the place that was home to them for so many years and move on. She went to Lodz. There, she met a young man from Vilna. They fell in love and got married. Rachel found out that she had an aunt in London and eventually she and her husband settled in England.

They worked hard and started a family. Unfortunately, Rachel's husband died a young man and Rachel had to provide for her family. It was not easy, but she made it. She gave her children a good education and made sure they were prepared for life. She succeeded again. Now they have children of their own. Rachel remarried, and she and her husband have a happy life together. They live in England, and for a couple of months every year, they go to Israel, where they have an apartment.

Here is a story of a young girl that went through so much before she found some happiness.

Lila Mazurowna-Margules

Was a quiet, rather pretty girl. She was a good student who took an active part in the social life of our class. Lila used to write for our class paper and many of her articles could be found in the "Student Forum." In general she was a swell girl, who had a lot of compassion for the poor and underprivileged Jewish children in Vilna. Here is the text of one of her articles about it:

"We, who live under comparatively good conditions, who live in large and warm rooms, who study in well-lit classrooms, have, however, to think of those children who are poor and deprived of all that. Their living standards and the conditions under which they study are most regrettable.

"So let us speak of the pupils of Jewish elementary schools, namely: the Sholom Aleichem School, the Dinenzon School for retarded children and the yeshiva (Jewish religious school). These are the schools we must help. But first of all, we have to know something about them.

"For this very purpose, the Board of our class delegated us to visit these schools. We will describe the things that we observed there. Let us start with the yeshiva. An old iron sign, half eaten away with rust, hangs on the gate. The sign reads: Jewish Religious School. We enter the yard. It is large. We see two synagogues and a small, one-story house. This is the yeshiva. Sons of poor parents are getting their education here. They sweat over the Torah, Mishnah and Gemara the whole day. Boys of different ages are sitting and studying with their rabbi.

"Most of them have pale and exhausted faces. It seems they are sad and depressed. Visitors are rare here. That is why our unexpected visit is such a pleasant surprise to them and they smile at us. It makes us feel good.

"Next, we go to the Sholom Aleichem School. Many of us know

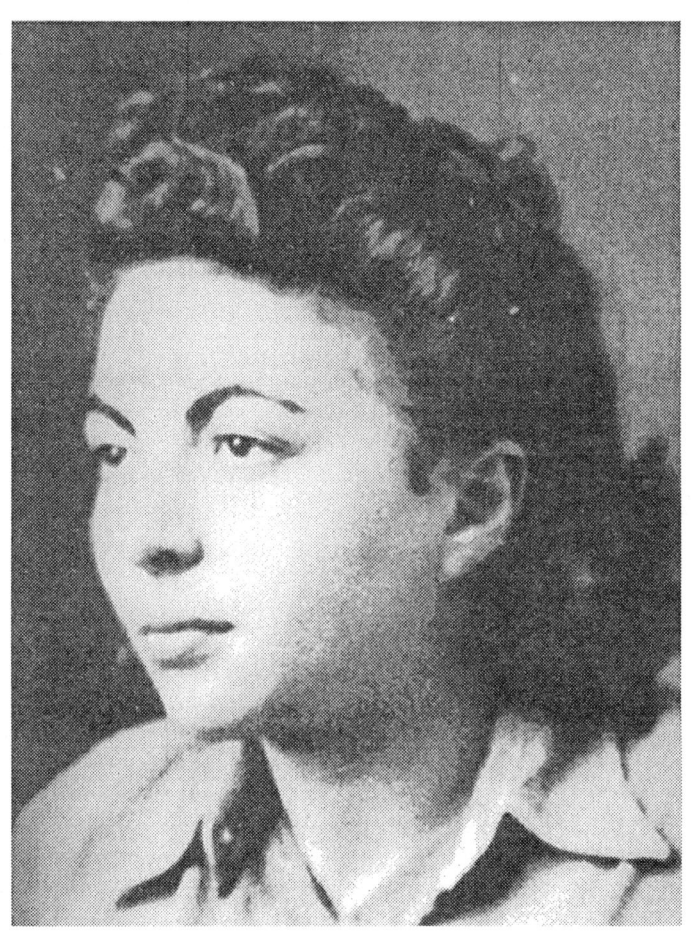

Lila Mazurowna

of this school, but not everyone had a chance to know it better. We will try our best to describe it to you. We see the dilapidated premises. We go upstairs to the classroom. Some noise comes from a distance. These are children going back home. We look attentively at them. These are children of various age and of various looks. But all of them are pale and undernourished. They wear shabby clothes. It is almost impossible to see a well-dressed child there. All of them are from the district of Novogrudska street. Their parents are poor and cannot pay much attention to them because they have to work hard. These kids live in small, one-room apartments and they have no place to prepare their homework. That is why their notebooks cannot be clean. It happens often that two or even three of them share one bed. Sometimes they are so poor that they have no money to buy food, let alone textbooks and notebooks.

"Maybe the time they spend at school is the most pleasant for them.

"Judge for yourself — must we take care of them or not, can we put up with this situation — that so many children live under such conditions?

"But this is not the end. Let us describe also the school for retarded children. The school is situated on Orzeszkowa Street. We enter the yard. Children point at a building that is not very big. We come in and ask for some information. The teachers receive us very well. They tell us the history of the school. It was founded in 1932, not long ago. The pupils interest us very much. They are mostly poor and defective children, some of them can read but they do it very slowly, others are afraid of everything. But there are some who have talent for music and drawing. We were shown their essays entitled 'My first day at school.' Some of them wrote very vaguely, others repeated one and the same sentence, but as a whole, their essays seemed to be correct, and it was very interesting for us to read them. We asked about the curriculum and were told that it was the same as in an ordinary elementary school, the only difference was that they spent two years more to complete it. There are fifteen pupils in a class, who are taught individually. The teachers thanked us for the clothes we brought, it was a present from our own school. They also asked us to bring gloves. We promised to deliver the gloves on our next visit.

"And now, when we have some information about our poor and ill colleagues, you will understand that it is necessary to come to their rescue. And the sooner the better" (see the article "Visiting school," 1938, No 9, pp. 14-15, joint authorship with S. Goldmanovna).

Such was the solidarity we expressed and the care we took of our indigent colleague pupils.

When I found out during my visit in New York that Lila was alive, I called on the phone in great excitement and we made a date to meet the next day at the library of the YIVO Institute. As I was sitting there and waiting, I suddenly saw a smartly dressed woman, rather tall and good looking, who was examining the faces of the visitors around her. More that fifty years had passed since we had seen each other. No wonder she did not recognize me. I called her name, she came over quickly and we greeted each other warmly as each of us thought: Is it really her? Is it really him? We decided to visit the Jewish Museum. As we walked slowly, she told me how she survived, what happened to her family. This is what she said: "I and my younger sister, Rachel (Raja) Mazur Sznajderhous, who was also a student in our school, are survivors of the Vilna Ghetto, Kaiserwald Concentration Camp (near Riga, Latvia), the Dunawerke Labor Camp, Stutthoff, and Steinhoff Labor Camp in East Prussia. We were liberated by the Russian tanks on March 11, 1945. Since our carefree childhood days, I had always been told: Lila, you are older, you have to take care of your little sister. This has stayed has with me my whole life. When the pink rosy bubble burst and the sad, dark days of the Nazi era came upon us, we lived through one tragedy after another. First we lost our young mother, then our father was taken our from the Ghetto pharmacy and sent to a labor camp in Estonia, then we were separated from our aunt Sonia (who was now our second mother) during the selection at the Rossa Cemetery the day of the liquidation of the Vilna Ghetto. Now we were two sisters all alone in the hostile world. As I look back at the long days of hunger and cold moral and physical persecution, I can see that the most dominant force in my battle to survive was the constant fear: What will happen to my little sister when I am not be there to take care of her? I assumed the role of the mother. After liberation, our roles reversed. We were both very sick for a very long time, but it took me longer to recover. Now she took care of me! Fed me, washed me, consoled me and brought me back to life. We were always together. The strong bond between us continues throughout our odyssey; through the displaced persons camps of Europe, after I got married, when we emigrated from Italy to Buenos Aires, Argentina, when she got married, when we started our own families. Even now, when we are far away from each other (I now live in New York) and cannot see each other as often as we wish, spiritually we are together now and forever."

Rachel Mazurowna

One of the many facts Lila told me about her past which especially stuck in my mind is: when in the Vilna Ghetto one day, she was taken to work with a group of girls to our school. They marched them toward the big cellar to sort out potatoes for the Gestapo, who occupied the whole building. As the column was moving toward the entrance, she saw Vincent, our school janitor and his two daughters standing right there and one of them exclaimed out loud: "Look, here is the little Lilka! I thought that all of those Jews were already killed at Ponary" Such were these people! When we were students and shared our lunches with them, they pretended to like us, to be our friends. Now they were showing who they really were. They enjoyed our misery instead of helping us.

Lila invited me for lunch. When we went into a restaurant and I saw the prices on the menu, I ran out. They were too high and she was treating me. We went into a pizza parlor, where we had a slice and a Coke. This she could do for me. From there, she phoned Vera Shapiro Toper, another classmate of ours, who also lived in New York.

Yulik Rafes

This is me, the author of this narrative. What can I tell you about my own self? I was very naive at that time, but I was a strong-willed person. I had been the class president for a number of years. I loved my classmates.

How naive and childish my school composition was if we look at it now. It was written at the language examination in 1932. I was eight then. "It happened in summer, at our summer cottage. I was eight then, and I used to be a great sweet-tooth, as every kid of this age is. I loved sweet things, especially sweet cream. One day, someone in the house bought a special liquid Sidol, for the purpose of cleaning door handles. This liquid was left on a small table in the kitchen. When I saw it on a plate, I immediately decided that it was custard. I ran to my Mom to ask for permission to eat it, but she was out. I thought that if I ate it, my mother would never become angry. That is why I went to the kitchen, took this so-called custard and tasted it. I got sick immediately and then vomited. When my parents returned and saw what had happened, they laughed for a long time. They were happy because I was punished for my gluttony, the result of which was a two-week illness. So, I was punished for my carelessness" (essay "A remarkable event in my life").

I, too, am alive today. I am writing these lines now and I think sincerely: "Why was I saved? For what merits? And is it at all possible to speak about who deserves to live? Can the chance to survive depend on the amount of someone's merits?"

I had only one so-called "merit." On June 22, 1941, at 11:30, my mother decided to leave everything and go east on a horse cart. So it was done. On June 23, it would have been too late. I went away by myself, by bicycle, and did not know where my parents were.

I started to work after school. I began my medical studies, then I met a person, a wonderful woman, beautiful, subtle, devoted, honest. So I met my future wife, whose whole essence was the continuation of the spirit of my school, my mates, I could always rely on her. It was as if she had always been studying together with me, all the time. It was a great happiness, but, sadly, she died in 1989 . . . She was better than me in every respect, I did not always take that into account, though, as she used to say, I always served as a stone wall for her. I had lived a happy life with her, though it was not that simple to become a doctor of medicine and chief of a gastrology clinic under such bad conditions, and I can say this is mostly her love and generosity that made it possible. I tried to preserve my human and national dignity. I can say that I succeeded.

She helped me in everything, supported all my ideas that could have seemed extravagant at first sight. And she supported me in the very idea that led to this very work you are reading now (be it successful or not). She appeared to be the star that lit all of my creative and professional paths and that continues to light all things that I am doing now. And it concerns also the writing of this, my work, which is not very big, but is very dear to me. I am living now in recollections about our school and about my wife. My life lost its attractiveness without her. She was my life.

My son took up all the best traits that she possessed: kindness, honesty, responsiveness, diligence, striving for perfection and care for the home and hearth, and . . . great emotional vulnerability. He takes care of me, and does his best. He has a good wife and a son.

My older sister Lala also attended our high school. She was an outstanding student. I remember vividly one episode. When I finished public school and was getting ready to enter high school. Mr. Morgenstern, who taught Polish language and literature, was reading our names from the school book in order to get to know us better. When it came to my name, he stopped and asked me if Lala Rafes from the eighth grade in the gymnasium was my sister. After my affirmative answer, he said, "It would be nice if you followed in her footsteps."

During the war, she was a nurse at the front and often while under

Lala Rafes

fire saved peoples' lives. Ambitious and dedicated, she had a hard life. Unfortunately, she is not with us anymore.

Abrasha Santocki

Then, unexpectedly, we found out that two of our schoolfellows lived in New York. They were Abrashka Santocki and Gabik Sedlis.

Being on a business trip, I directed my steps to the house where my best schoolmate lives... (Both were the best: he and Zalik Rudnicki). A good guy, responsive, devoted, anyone could rely on him. What a meeting it should be. More than fifty years had passed. We were children, now we are old men. We have lived our lives in different social formations. There is still a danger that we can meet as two people who are complete strangers to each other. It would hurt me. It would be even more painful, because of the lack of cordiality and the lack of kindness that I had suffered since my wife died. I myself became another person, life seemed senseless to me. I really did not know what to live for. It appeared that she was my life. Nothing could make me glad, I just existed, nothing else, and that is why I had to act somehow. In this very mood I was advancing on Abrashka's place. Many things faded away out of my memory, but I can still see some of them. The house emerges before my eyes, that very house, on Weglowa street (not near the corner), and common "kavaly" (jokes we played on our classmates).

We were so much alike. We presented a "troika" (trio) of inseparable friends (Abrashka, Zalik and me), very attached to each other. These things never slipped away from my memory.

It is stuck in my memory forever: the kaval (joke) that we made together with Abrashka. I could have been thrown out of my school for that joke. In Vilna, it is a custom to hold a street festival in honor of Saint Casimir. They hold this festival every year and it is named "Kazjuk" (this tradition is preserved even now). The festival was held on Lukishska Circle, right in the center of the city. There was a great variety of interesting things there: various works of folk craftsmen from the neighboring boroughs and country areas, native dishes, embroidery, carving, paintings, trinkets, toys and whatnot.

There was a toy there that drew our attention immediately. Let me describe it: the toy was named "a little barking dog." It was a small rubber ball that had a metallic head of a dog stuck on it. We bought five of them. Our plan was simple: to distribute these toys among pupils in the class. The next day, the plan was fulfilled. Of course, we had our own plants among the pupils, and the toys were given to them

Abrasha Santocki

only. Their duty now was to create loud "barking" during the lesson (do not forget now that the teacher of mathematics was a real threat). As for the rubber ball, it had to be placed under the plant's foot. But not to be squeezed in the hand — in that case, everyone would have seen it. We did it! I remember very well what was going on — the barking and the hullabaloo. The teacher could not understand what exactly was happening, so he suddenly addressed me (I was the class president). "Rafes, what does this barking mean?" I will never forget the mischievous expression on Abrashka's face, especially at the moment when he was looking at me, so curious and so eager to see the end of the story, namely, how on earth I was going to get out of this direct question. As for me, I did not in the least feel embarrassed. I simply pointed to the open window. We could see the school yard, it was April. "There are little dogs in the yard, barking," I said. The lesson was stopped. I was called out to the principal's office and then expelled for three weeks.

Cautiously, I directed my steps to Abrashka now. What if these fifty years that passed had left nothing for us to remember? No, it cannot be so.

I was right. I entered the room. I saw Abrashka, I saw his wonderful wife. And it seemed those fifty years of separation never existed.

I had a feeling as if I were not a middle-aged man, but that little boy from the Epstein–Szpeizer Gymnasium. I felt that I was near a person very close to me.

Abrashka's life was not an easy one. He survived the war in the Soviet Union. Right after the end he left and finally settled in the United States. When I came to visit, he was going through a very difficult period of his life. He was facing very serious illnesses of members of his immediate family. In spite of this, he showed a lot of courage and was a wonderful host.

What was most striking in Abrashka was his inexhaustible humor and kindness. He took so much interest in everything that concerned me. I had never before met a more responsive man. That simply disarmed me. He had been constantly trying to get me to say that I needed something from him. But my reply had been, "No, I do not need anything."

Acute mind, logical, and what counts more — boundless sincerity. He was successful in his life, but he did not say a word about that. Only by accident did I find out that he was an accomplished specialist in his field.

He was always joking, always kidding — he is a person, who has a strong sense of humor, and at the same time a serious and thoughtful analyst of all the things we were alarmed about. I will never forget his wife, Teresa. She is both beautiful and nice, and she is a very interesting person. One can feel at ease with her.

I never had a feeling that she stood aside, I perceived her somewhere near. I also had a feeling that she was one of our classmates, though she was naturally much younger. Teresa is from Vilna too.

Teresa had also gone though a lot, she hid in Nemenchiny, pretending to be a Polish child. After that she wandered through Lithuania, Poland, Germany, up to the moment when she at last found herself at Abrashka's place, in New York.

I cannot help saying the following: several years have passed since we met, but in spite of this fact, being far from Abrashka and living on another hemisphere, I constantly feel him to be near, I feel that he is always a devoted friend. He, in his turn, keeps on being interested in my life and offers his help. Here is a true friend, a friend from those years that seemed to be so distant. I think that only by being schoolmates can people keep such a close friendship.

Eli Santocki, the older brother of Abrasha Santocki, also attended our high school. He was four years older than us. We all knew him as a very famous athlete in football and hockey. After the war, he was one of the first to go to Israel.

Gabik Sedlis

I felt at ease at their place. An hour had not yet passed when Gabik Sedlis entered the room. It was the very first day of our get-together.

I remember him very well. He was a quiet boy, and who would have thought that he would be able to go through the ghetto, become a partisan and be a courageous fighter against our bitter enemy - the German army?

Gabik had not changed much. I think all people who are built slight preserve their young looks. Gabik brought his son with him, I gave him a scolding, "Why did he not answer my letters?" He did not feel hurt. He showed his photo to his son. It was a copy of the photo from the school days I had made for him. He was very glad to have it.

We had a good day, he showed me New York. We observed New York on board the excursion steamer. He told me about the ghetto, about how they bid farewell, he and his mother, who was later killed

Eli Santocki

Gabik Sedlis

by fascists. He was telling me all this and crying. Now he has a family. He has a wife and two children. He is an architect and has a business of his own. I was told that two more our classmates lived in New York: Lila Mazur Margules and Vera Shapiro Toper.

Gabik tells us:

"When the ghetto was set up in 1941, you could take with you only whatever you could carry. My father was a doctor in the Jewish Ghetto Hospital. He was absorbed in daily work, but never planned how to save his own family. Whatever happened to other Jews would happen to us. This was the thinking of the majority of intellectuals. We in the ghetto had to work for the Germans outside of it. I was seventeen and my big interest was art. Before the German invasion, I went to preparatory school for the Academy of Fine Arts. Now I worked as a sign painter.

"I painted and did graphic work. I got second prize in a painting contest. In those days, such things were keeping us alive. One of the most horrible things, besides being killed, was having your dignity taken away from you, so the cultural activities were very important. I also knew I had a limited amount of time before I would be killed. People told us about a place called Ponary outside Vilna, where Nazi **Einsatzgruppen** and their Lithuanian henchmen were killing the Jews. If there was an action and they took thousands of people, and you were left alive, you gave a sigh of relief: I made it. And the fact was, it may have been only for a few months.

"The resistance fighters were a very tight group, numbering only three hundred people. There were only three ways to be accepted: you belonged to a political youth organization, you possessed a weapon or you had some expertise. I belonged to no youth organization and owned no weapon. But I wanted very badly to join. My only expertise was drawing and this skill proved to be very useful. A young doctor who worked for my father had some cont acts with the Polish underground, the AK, and learned from them how they manufactured face identity papers. He needed an artist with graphic skills to draw stamps by hand, which were later imprinted on washed-out passports. I was recruited for this task. I forged one set of identity papers and shortly afterwards I was approached by Jacob Gens, who asked me to provide a false document for a relative. I did so, and the day after, I was contacted by the resistance. I was accepted into the resistance in the summer of 1943, fifty-two years ago. On the day of the final liquidation of the Vilna Ghetto, on September 23, 1943, I came to a meeting place prepared to fight. When I arrived, I saw that the few remaining machine guns were disassembled and ready to be transported. That's when I knew that we were not going to fight. I told my leader, Abba Kovner, that I did not bring along my forgery tools, and he ordered me to return home for them.

"That was last time I saw my mother. I told her that I was leaving the ghetto to fight in the forest, and she said she suspected as much and that it was the right thing to do, because a child has to survive a parent. I felt guilty about leaving her...

"I still do. She was forty-nine years old, and she gave me her life's wisdom. She said, 'I know that you are going to survive. Live life to the fullest. If you have money, it can be taken away from you, and if you have children, they can die, but no one can take away a life lived well.'

"We went out of the Ghetto through the sewers. We hurried to the forest, where we joined our colleagues who were fighting alongside Soviet-Lithuanian partisans. I remember the welcome speech we got: 'We welcome you here on the base. We know that until now, you have collaborated with our enemy. You can wash your hands of this treason by fighting. There is an enormous quantity of weapons, but they are in the hands of the Germans and you have to get them.'

"In July, 1944, we entered the city with the Soviet Army and fought in the streets of Vilna. This was our hour: children fighting for days with no sleep, starved but euphoric, all on adrenaline. On July 8, 1944, the Battle of Vilna ended. The Jewish partisans who left the Ghetto in 1943 to fight the Germans now returned to Vilna as liberators. Very soon after that, I had a talk with Abba Kovner, who said, 'Gabriel, we are organized, but we are not going to stay here working for the Soviets, we are going to emigrate to Palestine to build a Jewish home and try to help other Jews do likewise.' Later, in Lublin, Poland, Abba Kovner and the leaders of the resistance from other cities, including Warsaw, founded the organization called Briha, whose mission was to repatriate Jews to Palestine. I joined other partisans and worked for Briha until shortly after the war."

Gabik was lucky to meet and marry a warm and friendly girl, Joanna. They raised two wonderful, intelligent children. Joanna herself was in the Warsaw Ghetto.

Tania Spektorowna-Peter

Lila and Vera told me that several more of our classmates live in Israel: Tania Spektorowna, Borka Shub, Musia Levowna, Dodzka Kremer. I had gotten in touch with Tania Spektorowna. I remember her

Tania Spektorowna

Jakob Stolowicki

very well, her apartment was a place where we used to meet. Actually, it was the only place where boys and girls could come together, dance and socialize.

Tanka had traveled a long and hard path, she learned how tough life in Soviet Russia could be, she lived through hunger, and cold, the illnesses, the loss of her dear father. After the war, she married a survivor and settled in Israel. She has a daughter in New York. Recently she lost her husband. That is sad, but what to do? Tania, remember your apartment on Mickiewicz Street? I think all of us who remained alive owe you a lot. We must be grateful to you, because your place was the epicenter of our get-togethers in our childhood. It seems so far away, but at the same time so near and dear to us.

Jasha Stolowicki

Many years ago, I was absolutely sure that no one had survived the Nazi era, except for me, that everyone had been swallowed by the bloodthirsty dragon.

Jashka Stolovicki was the first one that I found. Let us now listen to him, to one of them:

"Summer. It means: the end of school year, the heat, the summer cottage, the beach and the river, but I was not lucky enough to enjoy the pleasures of country living. My mother had left for Paris, and my father, 'a business shark,' as one of his chums called him, said he had no time to spend with me. I stayed in the city, whether I wanted to or not. Fortunately, I had found out that the Maccabi Sports Club existed, and that it was such a marvelous place, where I could lie in the sun, swim in the wonderful swimming-pool and have all this pleasure for only fifty groszy per month. As you know, I have the title of a first-rate philosopher. There, I stopped being philosopher. Everything changed in my life and my fellow swimmers called me 'Bobra' (Beaver), not even a proper otter.

"The first two weeks passed. And they were two very monotonous weeks. Then I moved to Grzegorzew, where the famous glider pilot school was situated. For a long time I had been doing my best to enter this school. At last I succeeded. The first period of studies was not too pleasant: the 'gallows,' the jumps, etc. I felt sick at first, but later, as time went by, I managed to sit firmly in the armchair and turn the wheel rather energetically. My first flight was a success, it was unexpected, but I came back home with the 'A' category. But wait, two years later, you would see me be a candidate for the 'B' category.

"The second month flew by very rapidly. To kill time and to relieve monotony, I visited my colleague in Novye Verki.

"There, I had some picturesque impressions and even an adventure. This adventure could have had a fatal end. While fishing, I fell into the water and nearly drowned. Only due to my experience gained in Maccabi and also due to my nickname, which was 'Frog,' I coped with the situation and came out on the surface. As a result, I can assure you, that in spite of the fact that I stayed in the city in summer, I have spent my holidays more cheerfully that all of you. And I am glad and proud of that!!!" (essay "Holidays in the city," 1938).

Jashka named himself "The Philosopher Number One." He had a nickname, "Kvacher Kvok." He was given this nickname because the shape of his body resembled a duck.

I was sitting in my room at the hotel. The telephone rang.

"Yes?" I said. "Is this Giraffe?" (Giraffe was my nickname, because of my long neck). I immediately realized that it could be no one but a schoolmate on the other end of the line. I was right.

Jashka's life appeared to be very hard. He left Vilna on the very first day of the war. His parents stayed in the city. They were slaughtered. He fought during the second war, was wounded. He got married, had three kids. He had to work and could not go on with his studies. But working as an engineer, he succeeded in every respect. He took an active part in work concerning medical engineering and space exploration problems. Since that time, since 1950, I have often met him in Vilna. Highly educated, with a great store of knowledge, a man of a particular mentality, a person of ready sympathy, benevolent, exclusively tolerant and optimistic in his relations with people, forgiving people all their drawbacks and vices. He is an extraordinary person in every respect.

At school, he was notable for his two hobbies: glider piloting and fishing. He is an inveterate fisherman, and fishing remains his hobby to this day. He never complains, but to me the most important thing in him is that he is a friend. I cannot accept everything in him, there are some things that I do not like, but he is mine, he is my own. He is mine in the days of mirth, and in the days of my mortal grief (the passing of my wife), he was at my side. No words. We are not bound by any business — we are bound by our school years. He had always been in high spirits when he visited Dnepropetrovsk, always (notwithstanding all the difficulties and obstacles in life, and there were many). We had been sitting in the room all night (my wife Dusia had already fallen asleep). We had been drinking, and that night was devoted to memories of our childhood, of our class.

I remember, we put down all the names, and with great bitterness and pain we thought of the misfortune that befell them. And we thought, no one had survived.

Vera Shapiro Toper

Verka always been a small and brisk girl to us, and always well-wishing. We called her and half an hour later, she was in the street, a young woman, joyful, active, optimistic. She did well at school. She liked Thomas Edison's biography. It was she who wrote in her school composition: "The childhood of Thomas Edison was not as colorful as the childhood of children of other social status. His father, who was a used-clothes man, was not able to feed his large family. That is why Thomas had to earn his living. Thomas Edison was a worker in the goods wagon, he spent the money he earned buying books. The rest of the money was always sent home. At a young age, he took a great interest in science, which is why he studied different books so diligently. His passion for books increased even more when the librarian in Detroit told him that studies were a clue to the world. Thomas Edison invented special roller skates for luggage. This invention could save time and work. Edison's second invention was a bell connected to a lock, and it rang when the train approached the station. Thomas saved the life of a child of a railroad man and as a result, he got a job at the telegraph office. That was the place where he could demonstrate his abilities, his passion for inventions. Eventually, he invented an electric bulb. And we use his electric bulb in our flats up to now. He died recently, but his name will always remain in the soul of mankind" (essay "I read about a nice person").

This essay was written by a young girl. Everything changed when she was 17. This is what Verka told me in New York.

"So much changed in our lives. The War ruined our entire youth. I was the only one from our family who survived. When the Germans entered Vilna, we were taken to the ghetto, we were there until 1943. When this ghetto was liquidated, we were sent to different camps. We found ourselves again in Poland at the end of the war, near Gdynia, and there we were liberated by the Russians. Under their guidance, on March 11, 1945, I began to work with captives (Englishmen, Italians, Frenchmen). We prepared new documents for them to enable them to go back home.

When the war in Europe ended, I left Poland for Germany, Holland, Belgium and France. When I was in France, I found out that my mother's sister and brother were in America. I lived in Paris until

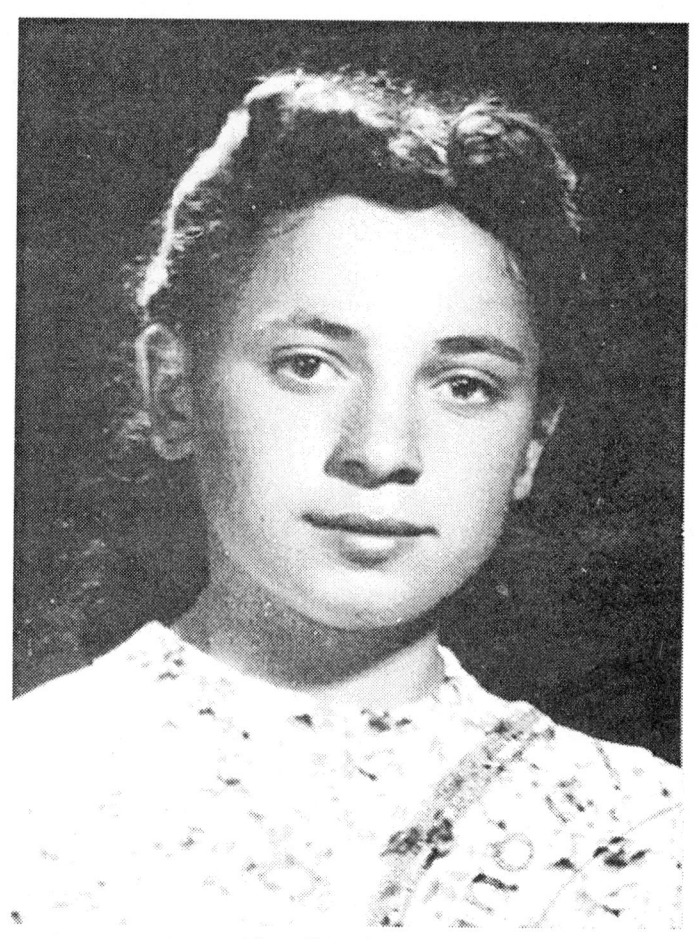

Vera Shapirowna

the beginning of 1946 and then left Paris for America, where I lived at my aunt's place. I went to school to study English. Human nature can adapt to anything. I was able to start a new life after those four years of horror, hunger and humiliation. In 1947, in June, I married Sam. We have just celebrated our forty-seventh wedding anniversary. Sam used to live in China, he came back to the United States when he was twenty-three to enter university. He was called up for military service in the U. S. Army. He worked as an interpreter in Russian, Chinese and French. After the war, he returned to his university, where he received a doctorate in economics. As for me, I worked for more than forty years for a chocolate company. I supervised shops. Now I am retired, but sometimes I work."

She has a son and a daughter-in-law. She is satisfied with her life. This is how things are now for this fragile and quiet girl, our schoolmate Vera. Regardless of what she experienced during the war, Vera remained sensitive and very responsive to people's needs with a positive and optimistic outlook on life. It is really amazing that after losing her entire family so tragically, she possesses such sensitivity and warmth for people and is very much dedicated to the memory of our perished friends.

The Epstein–Szpeizer Gymnasium was a very progressive school. It was always adopting the best available system in education in the middle thirties. It adopted a French-system lycee. Before the change, there were four classes in grade school and eight classes in high school. In the new system, there were six classes in grade school, four classes in high school and two classes in the lycee. The lycee gave us two choices, you could pick the humanities or the science department. The first class to graduate from the lycee was in the year 1939.

That was the year that Henry Shapiro, the older brother of Vera Shapiro Toper, finished high school.

"I will never forget the joy, happiness and the expectation we shared in June of 1939. Our whole future was ahead of us. None of us expected that in September of the same year, our world would collapse around us.

"I adored my brother, he was my best friend. He protected me and he guided me. He instilled in me the thirst for knowledge, the love of books. He opened my mind and my eyes to all that is beautiful in this world. He was planning to go to study in the United States, but the war changed everything. He attended Stefan Batory University of Vilna.

"June of 1941 brought the beginning of the end. It is much too painful to dwell on this period. I lost my brother in 1944 in the

Henry Shapiro

Holocaust. This loss left a vacuum in my heart which I never was able to fill. Now, more than half a century later, there is not a single day that I do not think of him. Everytime I see something beautiful, I think of him and I would love to share it with him.

"He was one of many wonderful young students who could have given so much to make this world a better place, but they never had a chance. They were destroyed in the prime of their life for only one reason. They were Jewish.

"They perished, but they are not forgotten. They live in us and our children."

Sonia Zakladowna

A small quiet little girl, with a reddish tint in her hair, pleasant face with a lovely smile. She lived with her mother and her older sister on Wivulski, on the first floor. Many students going to our gymnasium had to pass by her house and often we saw her in the window looking out. Like everyone else, her life was changed by the war. Her family was taken to the ghetto. Who would have thought that this little quiet girl will become a partisan fighting against German soldiers. She survived the war and settled in Israel. She came to the United States and started a new family. Her life was not an easy one, but she lived a full life with many devoted friends. We are saddened today that in April of 1996, she passed away after a long illness. She was popular and very friendly and we will miss her.

Noema Shilanska

She was one of the most beautiful girls in our class, everyone yearned for her. She was a blond and had blue eyes, she was tall, slim and self assured, and was a candidate to become Miss of the Class, she was slightly supercilious and sure that she was the best. What happened to her? She was seen in Italy by the Sedlises, but I don't know her whereabouts now.

And this is what she said in her school composition "Getting about town at night":

"I am going home from the movies after seeing a tragic drama. The street is crowded with noisy passing cars and cabs. It is the throbbing of the pulse of life. Shop windows and signpost boards are brightly lit and cast their bright light at people, who are hurrying, always nervous, excited and preoccupied. As for me, I feel like a little girl in such a crowd. I am embarrassed. I do not know where to direct

Noema Shilanska

my step. The city is swirling, music can be heard from the open windows, from houses and bars. A light breeze touches my face gently, caressing my hair playfully.

"The night life will start in a moment. Beautiful limousines will stop near the cafe. Quite suddenly, darkness embraces the city.

"I can hear the clock quietly striking from the nearest church. The clock strikes the hour. The city becomes calm, the night embraces it with its dark blanket as if it were a small child. Lanterns are glimmering with their dull yellow light.

"The wind grows stronger, the branches of trees are swinging, a small drizzling rain is coming down. I get into the maze of narrow small lanes that are surrounded by old walls.

"Shabby houses cast their shadows on the street, and a small patch of the sky becomes invisible. It is absolutely empty around, and only the awful shout of alarm and horror can be heard from time to time from the nearest pub. After that everything is quiet again. The night watchman armed with his stick and his keys goes around singing a song in a hoarse voice.

"The rain grows stronger and stronger. The wind is howling, I can hear how the rain is pelting down on the windows. That is why I am going back home."

Noema Shilanska's mother died when Noema was a very little girl. Her father, a tall, handsome man, brought her up with her two older sisters. She began her studies in a Hebrew school. She came to Epstein-Szpeizer much later and right away became very popular in our class.

Boris Shub

I wrote a letter to Bor'ka in Israel. I received his reply, but not immediately. Half a year later, I saw him in Vilna, he came with a delegation to Ponary for the inauguration of the memorial to those hundred thousand Jews who were killed during the war. It is the place where the parents of many of our classmates lie, who were saved by a miracle. Bor'ka's parents were also shot there. He told me about the ghetto, about how he met Yalik Merlis. He was a true genius, this Yalik; he was gentle and vulnerable, and that is why he was doomed from the start in the ghetto. He told me about Jacob Kushkin (Kukus), what a wonderful guy he was.

I looked at Bor'ka as he told me about all these incredible sufferings, about the death of his sister, who refused to undress before being shot and after she had been beaten for that, she spat in

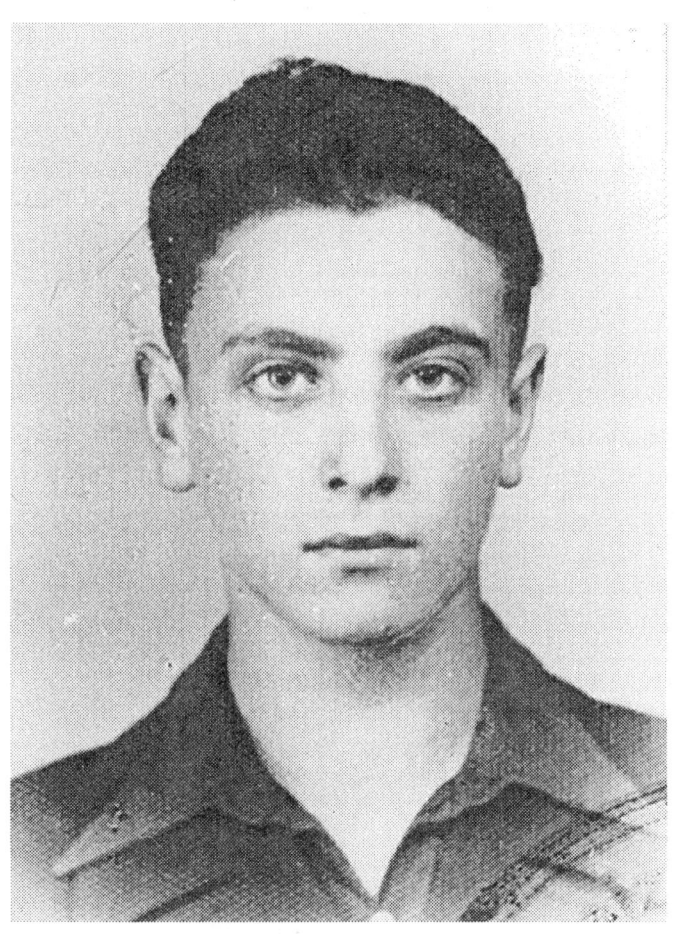

Boris Shub

the face of her executioner. She was shot on the spot. He was saved by a miracle, because he escaped to the forest and joined a partisan detachment. He went through the war, he became an aviation engineer, he is still working, is married and has two sons. He himself calls them "Herculeses."

I showed him a photo which I had kept from our schooldays. "Who is that?" he asked me. "It is you," I answered, "Can it be so?!"

And now I saw a tall, middle-aged man, who looked like a military man. He was so quiet as a schoolboy. He used to be our goalkeeper. So quiet, yet he proved to be so courageous, never broken and looking ahead with optimism, in spite of the fact that he experienced so much tragedy. At the same time, he is capable of looking back and his attitude about the past is marked by tender sentimentality.

We were not so much attached to each other as we were with Abrashka. But those several days that we spent together were full of warmth, kindness and attention to each other. And they are unforgettable.

He wrote and published, in Hebrew, a very interesting autobiography about his whereabouts and achievement during his life span. It makes very interesting reading. We can add one more fact to his credit, he fought bravely for Israel's independence.

Luba Kaganovich

"I have so many wonderful memories about my life before the war. One can never forget marvelous those high school days. The memorable trip we took to Warsaw, Cracow, Wieliczka and Zakopane. Winter in Vilna, the skating rink right in our school yard. Springtime and the classes that were conducted in our school garden. The fear before a math test with professor Fesel.

"Our carefree life ended on June 22, 1941. That day, I was sailing on the Vilia River and the Germans started to bomb the city.

"For the first two months, we were home. In the beginning of September, we were taken to the Ghetto. While in the Ghetto, I was lucky to work for the Wehrmacht and not for the Gestapo, and I was treated fairly. At the end, I was taken to work in a place where they fixed cars. The man in charge knew about the liquidation of the Ghetto and organized a camp for his workers which was not in the Ghetto. Unfortunately, I was not able to take my family with me. My father and my thirteen-year-old brother were deported to Finland. Luckily, my sister and my mother were able to get into the same camp. We were together for nine months. Life was not easy. Children and old people were taken away and killed. We were able to make up our mother so she looked much younger then she actually was. We were lucky to save her from death.

"On July 9, the Germans began to retreat. We hid in a place underground. There were eighty of us. We were there for four days in terrible conditions. The Russians entered the city and saved us.

"One can write endlessly about our life. We paid a tremendous price. Our victory is that we produced a new generation and we know that their life will be better and easier than ours."

We were happy to find out that Bluma Blondesowna, Musia Lewowna and Lila Sakierowna, who were at one time in our class, survived the war and settled in Israel.

May 1990. Yulik Rafes, Lily Mazur-Margules,
Vera Shapiro-Toper, Abrasha's wife Theresa,
Abrasha Santocki and Gabik Sedlis
in Abrasha Santocki's apartment in New York.

EPILOGUE

Dear Reader!

You have just finished reading the last page of this story. I am afraid it is rather presumptuous of me to call it a story. It is rather a collection of observations and essays written by the students of the Epstein-Szpeizer Gymnasium about themselves, their lives, their dreams and their school days.

The specific feature of this documentary work is that the author himself, being a pupil of the school described, had found in the archives some documents related to our school activities, articles and essays of our pupils that had been published in the school magazine. This was a special mode of narration: not only to give my personal recollections, but to use my schoolmates in this work. They spoke themselves, that is why pupils and teachers who are presented here are alive in this book.

Of course, the literary delivery in these school essays is not very clear cut. But I did my best to preserve the language and the spirit of the original as far as my literary knowledge and interpreting abilities enabled me to do that.

You will not find very many comments of my own here, as well as perceptions. If there are some, they are made as a summary. Of course, these are not memoirs, memoirs were not my aim. Life at the Jewish school in the Lithuanian Jerusalem is presented not like recollections of modern contemporaries, but shown by pupils of those days. These pupils do not live in the author's reminiscences (which are mostly blurred by the passing of time), but they live by themselves in the school life of those days. Usually, an author recalls the past and writes today, when a long period of time has already gone by. And, willingly or unwillingly, "the now" of reality today, separates him from the reported events and influences to some extent the material provided.

So, as a result, sometimes we do not get from the text the reflection of the true reality of those days with its true aspirations, thoughts, worries and desires.

You have met the teachers of my school, and maybe you can feel now not only the things that united them (high pedagogical qualification, the knowledge of foreign languages), but you can also feel that all of them had traveled a long hard path in order to become outstanding teachers. They suffered material hardship, all of them earned their living by also giving private lessons. The students also worked hard at school and helped their families with money in spite of their young age. As a rule, it was like that:

The school's self-government, Self Help, was of special importance. This self-government did much for pupils, so that they could develop their habits of self-dependence, a knowledge of nature, their talents and hobbies and as a result, the moral and spiritual potential grew wider and wider.

The unique result of the pupils' self-government was a printed newspaper-magazine that was issued 1935-1939. On its pages, all the nuances of the exciting and dynamic school life were reflected. One can find here the information about studies as well as the information concerning pupils' relations in class, both descriptions of the self-government and material critical of their work, and also descriptions of cultural and political life of the city, of the country, of the world. There are lines here devoted to the Jewish problem, and they occupy a special place. There is and there was an opinion among Vilna Jewish society (some part of it) that our secondary school was a school inclined to assimilation. This was not true. The articles on the Jewish subject refute this opinion. Material about the Jewish Vilna, about writers, religious workers, cultural workers, Zionist politicians, articles, dreams of their own state, all that obviously shows that the Jewish spirit and Jewish national mentality of the pupils at the Epstein School was no less than the national mentality of other schools that taught in Yiddish or Hebrew.

It is clearly seen at the same time that they had been brought up to be respectful and attentive to the needs and wishes of other people.

They appear before us as any other school children of any other people and continent, being curious, restless, romantic and naughty.

Actually, they had everything ahead of them (they were only youngsters), all of life with its grief and joy, wins and losses was ahead of them, as well as the happiness of being a mother and a father. They had dreams as all kids in the world had, they had hopes for future success in life. Many dreamed of their future, of scientific accomplishments. They aspired to the summit of knowledge and wanted to master different professions.

They had the right to all that, not less than other children in the world. It was a simple human right, the right which was given by God, by Nature itself, by the all-human notion of "humanism" and all-human understanding of a person as it is, things that we now call "civil rights" or "human rights."

Nothing, it seems, could distinguish them from pupils of their age at any other school. They studied, they debated and created, they were naughty. They received different grades at school — from very good to failing. They united and created a pupils' organization, they went on excursions, fell in love, issued a printed newspaper which was unique even for those days. They were authors as well as reviewers. Everything was the same as in other schools in other countries. They, these pupils, did not differ from the rest of the world. But they were Jews who lived at the time when being Jewish was considered a crime. They belonged to that part of mankind that gains the notion of the image of enemy at every possibility for that historical period, and under the direction of the ruling clique. This "image of the enemy" is so convenient and simple at the same time. And so tragic for the victims are regimes that cast doubt on the very right of a person to live, that determine the right to live by the color of your skin and by your race and religion. These regimes determine who has this right to live and who has not, and do it with heartless cruelty. It was the fascist, racist regime that deprived these Jewish children of their right to live.

And they, as a rule, looked ahead at their future with optimism and hope.

All that was natural for their age, could it be any other way? But things turned for the worst. Most of them were killed, murdered without pity.

You have read their simple stories, stories of pupils of one school only, and you could look closely at their young and beautiful faces, the faces of fourteen- to seventeen-year-old girls and boys, children that only began their way in life. You can feel now what they lived by, what they dreamt about. I am absolutely sure (in any case I hope), that you, my dear reader, will never remain indifferent to their tragic destinies.

We do not only pay homage to those who perished. This work has its own teaching value. Nothing is added by me. I give only bare facts. It is a documentary, a narrative where real people speak for themselves. Nothing has been invented by the author! And every pupil, every teacher and director can find for himself many things that are of importance today. But the main thing (and it would be my dream come true) is the importance of a pedagogical upbringing in which the seeds of non-acceptability of national hatred and intolerance, the seeds of respect for every nation would be planted at the very beginning.

This is the fight for the greatest right of every person — the right to live. The majority of pupils of my school were deprived of that right.

It is natural, however, that the author could not present here all the pupils of the school mentioned above, neither those who perished nor those who survived. Fortunately, our class is preserved much more fully.

It is possible, and I do not exclude this possibility, that many "Epstein pupils" would like to write their own notes, appendixes, memoirs of this school after they have read this very book. Many would like to write about their own life path. We would be grateful to all of them. And maybe a second edition of this book will be possible. Of course, it is a dream.

You have read this book and please do not judge the author too strictly. For the author is but an ordinary Epstein student, an "Epsteinjak."

Dear reader! Our wish is that everyone who has read this book could feel the reverential necessity to bend his head in the memory of these young lives.

Let their images never fade away out of your memory. Let this tragedy of Jewish youngsters, which happened to them in the middle of the twentieth century, never be repeated in any nation!!!

Realize clearly the necessity and importance to continue the steady struggle with these evils — racism, chauvinism, anti-Semitism.

APPENDIX
DOCUMENTS FROM ARCHIVES

WILNO

Wilno.

Pięć liter. Cały wyraz ułożony jakąś tajemniczą, niewidzialną ręką. Dla jednego człowieka coś, dla drugiego nic. Dla mnie.. wszystko.

Od pierwszego dnia mego życia słyszę ten sam wyraz. W różnym czasie jednak miał on różne brzmienie. Raz słuchałam tego słowa beztrosko, raz smutna, rozgoryczona do dna, raz z uśmiechem na ustach. Raz zdawało mi się, że ten wyraz zawiera w sobie coś dużego, ogromnego, nie mającego kresu i nie mogącego być pomieszczonym w granicach żadnego ludzkiego rozumu, raz zaś, że ten wyraz zawiera w sobie coś małego, bliskiego mi, że to „coś" potrafię zmieścić w sobie samej, już nawet tkwi we mnie głęboko, głęboko i... mocno.

O każdej godzinie widzę Wilno innym — a jednak zawsze takim samym. O w pół do ósmej z przepływającym tłumem robotników, dążących do jednego celu, a śpieszących w różnych kierunkach. Wszyscy podobni są do siebie, a jednak tak różni. Mali, zgarbieni, wtuleni w strzępy ojcowskich ubrań, bohaterowie — marzący o śniadaniu w szkole — uczniowie powszechnej. Więksi, zadowoleni, rozmawiający o kinie, teatrze — uczniowie gimnazjum. O twarzach bladych, wynędz-

Doc. 1. Beginning of the article written by Chaia Trevisowna.

Doc. 2. Application from Chaim Epstein to the Department of Education for permission to open a new school.

Doc. 3. Application from Chaim Epstein to the Department of Education asking for permission to open a 8 grade Jewish gymnasium in the Polish language

Doc. 4. Letter from Chaim Epstein to the department of Education asking that uniforms from Epstein High School should be sold only to the students of that school

Gyvenimo aprašymas.

Детство провел в дальней, заброшенной деревушке, в Западной Украине и учился дома под руководством старшей сестры. Из-за отсутствия средств посещал школу только 3 года (III, IV, V классы гимназии), в остальных классах держал экзамены в качестве экстерна. В 1917 г. кончил гимназию и сейчас был мобилизован. Служил один год в австро-венгерской армии. В 1918 г. принял должность учителя в малом местечке и там работал до 1921 года. В течении трех лет не мог поступить в университет, ибо принимали только тех, которые служили в польской армии как добровольцы. Только в 1921 г. удалось попасть в университет на гуманитарный факультет и в этом году получил в Вильне должность учителя в частной гимназии, где работал до июня 1940 г. Несмотря на очень тяжелые обязанности в школе (12-13 часов работы в сутки), занимался по ночам сам и сдал 11 государственных экзаменов, но посещать лекции университета из-за отсутствия времени.

Doc. 5. The Questionnaire of M. Morgenstern

Doc. 6. Application to the Department of Education for permission to establish a students organization "Self-Help"

Doc. 7. Information about the work done by "Self-Help" in 1934-1935

Bratnia Pomoc obejmuje następujące sekcje:

1/ Sekcja Dramatyczna, do której należy także chór.

2/ Sekcja Kół Naukowych; w b.r.szk.są czynne koła: polonistyczne, filologji klasycznej, germanistyczne, historyczne, krajoznawcze /kurs poznania Wilna/ i fizyczne.

3/ Sekcja Sportowa /własna ślizgawka, wypożyczalnia sprzętu sportowego posiada 22 pary nart, 10 par saneczek i inne/.

4/ Sekcja Spółdzielcza; posiada sklepik szkolny.

Bratnia Pomoc urządza co tydzień świetlice, na których jest czynna czytelnia czasopism, wygłasza się referaty i odbywają się dyskusje na tematy aktualne. Posiada również wypożyczalnię podręczników szkolnych, z których korzystają niezamożni uczniowie przeważnie zupełnie bezpłatnie, lub za nieznaczną opłatą.

JUTRZENKA UCZNIOWSKA

JEDNODNIÓWKA.

Wydawnictwo „Bratniej Pomocy" Koedukacyjnego Gimnazjum Humanistycznego C. EPSZTEJNA w Wilnie.

Wilno, kwiecień 1925 r.

Nasz cel.

Naszym celem jest rozwój poczucia wspólności interesów między uczniami i zamiłowanie piękna.

Wychodząc z tego założenia, będziemy poświęcali w naszych jednodniówkach dużo miejsca sprawozdaniom z kółek, stowarzyszeń i organizacyj samopomocowych. Będziemy popierać uczciwą, cichą i owocną pracę dla dobra ogółu; obowiązkiem naszym będzie tępić demagogję, nieuczciwość, protekcję i inne wady pracy społecznej na terenie szkoły naszej i szkół wileńskich.

Piękno jest bodźcem do pracy i celem samo dla siebie. Dbali o zgodę i harmonję formy i treści, będziemy drukować artykuły teoretyczne o pięknie i jego znaczeniu, również chętnie będą widziane prace literackie uczniów.

Głównem zadaniem jest nawiązanie kontaktu z ogółem uczniów naszej i innych szkół. Wszystko, co drukować będziemy, chcemy czerpać nie z nielicznej i odosobnionej grupy, lecz z całej szkoły i dlatego wzywamy wszystkich do czynnej współpracy w naszem czasopiśmie, do rozpowszechnienia go—a placówka nasza, której hasłem jest praca i piękno, stanie na pewnym gruncie.

O naszej „Bratniej pomocy" i o pomocy wogóle.

Zarzuty. W ostatnich czasach coraz częściej spotykamy się z zarzutami, czynionemi naszej „Bratniej Pomocy". Większość zarzutów powstaje wskutek nieobeznania z jej powstaniem i funkcjonowaniem. Inne zarzuty są natury głębszej nie tyle w treści zarzutu ile w przyczynie.

Nasze zadanie. „Bratnia Pomoc" przy naszem gimnazjum istniała już w roku szkolnym 1922-23. W roku natomiast szkolnym 1923-24 nie wywołała w uczniach dość zainteresowania, i nie było nawet myśli jej zorganizowania. Dopiero w roku bieżącym 1924-25 powstała znowu o zakresie działania znacznie odmiennym.

Zwykłe zadaniem „Bratniej Pomocy" jest wspieranie materjalne uczniów. Uczniowie składają się względnie ofiarują swoją pracę na rzecz niezamożnych kolegów: płacą za nich wpisowe, dostarczają im książek, ubrania, pożywienia. Potrzeby umysłowe uczniów są odsunięte, bo nauczyciele i dyrekcja mają je zaspokoić, organizując kółka naukowe, względnie artystyczne.

W naszej „Bratniej Pomocy" sprawa ma się inaczej. P. Dyrektor gimnazjum i Komitet Rodziców, podjęli się zaspokoić potrzeby materjalne uczniów. Natomiast własną pracą mamy zorganizować zaspokajanie naszych potrzeb umysłowych. I trzeba zaznaczyć, że lepiej na tem wyszli p. dyrektor i rodzice, bo mają „tylko płacić", my zaś, uczniowie, sami mamy (co prawda, pod kierownictwem naszych profesorów) pracować nad udoskonaleniem się wewnętrznem swojem i swoich kolegów, umysłowem i moralnem.

Wychowanie moralne. Szczególnie trudne jest wychowanie moralne. Albowiem, jeśli nie zawsze się udaje wyćwiczyć, udoskonalić umysł (pracowali nad tem ludzie w ciągu kilku tysięcy lat), wcale innem jest zagadnieniem udoskonalenie duszy ludzkiej „wewnętrznego w człowieku anioła". I nad duszą pracowali ludzie od stworzenia świata, lecz podobno nie tak, jak nad umysłem. Przecież tylko kultura ludzka wzrosła i rozwinęła się w niesłychany sposób, cywilizacja tylko „kroczyła" naprzód, dzieje jednak zostawiając tysiące luk, przez które znowu wlewała się trucizna zwierzęcości. Szczególnie palącem stało się zagadnienie wychowania moralnego w naszych czasach, kiedy rodzice po większej części przestali zajmować się wychowaniem dzieci, sądząc, że po to istnieje szkoła: nauczyciel natomiast nie zawsze może wychować (nie „nau-

Doc. 8. Front page of the student paper "Student's Dawn"

— 204 —

Jednodniówka. Dnia ...... Cena 40 gr.

NASZA MYŚL

WYDAWNICTWO „BRATNIEJ POMOCY" KOEDUKACYJNEGO GIMNAZJUM HUMANISTYCZNEGO O. EPSZTEJNA W WILNIE

WILNO　　　　　　　MAJ　　　　　　　1929

OD REDAKCJI.

Oto macie przed sobą zbiorowy wyraz naszych pragnień, dążeń i ideałów, „Naszą Myśl" młodocianą, zdrową i jasną. Przez długi czas tkwiła ona głęboko w mózgach, śpiąca i nieświadoma siebie, aż ją wydobyliśmy i skrystalizowaliśmy. Pobudziliśmy do życia te siły twórcze, które w określonych granicach programu szkolnego nie mogły sobie znaleźć ujścia, a które w nas tkwiły potencjalnie. Apel nie przebrzmiał bez echa: pomógł przezwyciężyć wrodzoną bezwładność i niechęć do wyładowania energji i przemienić moc potencjalną w siłę żywą. Teraz jednak kiedyśmy przełamali pierwsze „nieczułe lody", kiedyśmy uświadomili sobie swą samodzielność duchową, swą zdolność do wcielania własnych, oryginalnych myśli w słowa, nie spocznijmy na pierwszych, skromnych laurach. Niech każdy z nas składa swój dorobek myślowy we wspólnej skarbonce, by móc potem — w przyszłości — dowoli z niej czerpać.

Razem młodzi przyjaciele!

Razem nieśmy wyzwolenie wszystkim siłom swej duszy, tajnym, śpiącym gdzieś w ukryciu, a niepobudzonym do życia nauką szkolną. Zestrzelmy myśli w jedno ognisko, by wysnuć z nich naszą wspólną, młodą Myśl. Pracujmy i wierzmy, że „Nasza Myśl" stanie się składnicą naszej wiedzy i kultury, a zarazem dźwignią i rękojmią przyszłego rozwoju, że dopomoże nam do zgłębienia samych

R. ZARĘCKA (kl. VI-b).

* * *

Często mówicie: praca z marzeniami!
Pocóż uciekać w świat cudów?
Pocóż za szczęściem gonić myślami,
Aby znów wrócić do brudów?
By rzeczywistość była straszniejsza
Po złotych snach, co się śniły?
By noc wokoło coraz ciemniejsza
Jeszcze się więcej ściemniła?
A gdyby nawet coś z dwojga gorszej:
Czy po przebytych cierpieniach,
Po dniu nużącym o nocnej porze
W słodkich odpocząć marzeniach?
Czy też by truły posępne troski?
Do jakich krwawe łzy łączyć?
Wyciągać straszne na przyszłość wnioski
I rany na nowo jątrzyć?
— Jeśli los duszę szarpie boleśnie,
Ściga oddechem swym mściwym,
Czemuż się nie śmiać przynajmniej we śnie?
Czuć się choć chwilkę szczęśliwym?
A gdy już chęć do marzeń odpada,
Dusza znużona jest zbytkiem wrażeń!
O biada temu, o stokroć biada!
Kto nie jest zdolny do marzeń!

siebie, do poznania psychologji kolegów i koleżanek i w rezultacie do nawiązania z pokrewnymi sobie stosunków umysłowych. Wierzymy wreszcie, że zbiorowy wysiłek rozwinie nasze predyspozycje duchowe, popchnie „bryłę naszego świata na właściwe tory", aż wyzwolimy w sobie wszystkie nieznane i śpiące moce, aż „Nasza Myśl" stanie się integralną cząstką Wielkiej Myśli Ludzkiej, aż dojdziemy per aspera ad astra!

S. Zelikson.

Doc. 9. Front page of the student's paper "Our Thought"

Rok II.   LUTY — 1936 r.   Nr. 1 (2).

FRONT
.| UCZNIOWSKI

Organ „Bratniej Pomocy" uczniów
Gimnazjum C. Epszteina i I. Szpajzera.

Sala Smuglewicza.
(Do artykułu „Bibljoteka Uniwersytecka").

Cena egzemplarza 30 gr.

Doc. 10. The title page of the paper "Student Forum"

Ukazanie się „Frontu Uczniowskiego."

Ukazał się pierwszy numer „Frontu Uczniowskiego". W pierwszym dniu gazetka była rozchwytana. Była sensacją, atrakcją, o której wszyscy mówili. Wszyscy na przerwach spacerowali z „F. U." w ręku. „Pilni" porzucili swoje stałe zajęcie na przerwach przepisywania czy też uczenia się lekcyi i czytali gazetkę. Ludzie o wojowniczych nastrojach zaprzestali na jeden dzień wojny, porzucili swoją amunicję, ogryzki papieru, i czytali gazetkę. Kto, jak kto, ale p. Wincenty musiał być napewno zadowolony z wydania gazetki. Zadowoleni zresztą byli wszyscy. Jeden mniej, drugi więcej, ale gazetka się spodobała.

Kupowali prawie wszyscy, w każdym bądź razie większość. fakt — nakład 400 egz.

W dniu ukazania się gazetki chciano urządzić święto „Św. Gazetego" i nie uczyć się. Nie udało się. Czy ukazała się gazetka, czy nie ukazała, ty męczenniku nauki, dwóje dostawaj. Trudno, ale na szczęście ta nieudała próba nie zniechęciła czytelników i nie przyczyniła się do zmiany stosunku do „Frontu Uczniowskiego". Stosunek pozostał ten sam—przyjacielski. Jeszcze lepiejby było, gdyby stosunek był aktywnoprzyjacielski. To znaczy przysłanoby więcej artykułów. Prawda, i teraz skarżyć się nie można, ale jeszcze więcej wcale nie zaszkodziłoby.

W pierwszych dniach można było słyszeć dużo rozmów o gazetce, ogólne wrażenie: wszyscy szczerze się śmiali, czytając „Żywot ucznia". Ludzie dziwili się i mówili: no, zobaczcie, i Rej na coś może się przydać. Trochę sensacyj wywołał wywiad z dyr. Szpakiewiczem. Podniosło to naszą dumę „narodową" (narodu uczniowskiego).

Uczniowie to też niebyle kto. Nawet taki artysta, jak p. dyr. Szpakiewicz, zadaje się z nami. Także wiersze się spodobały. Tu już duma „narodowa" doszła do szczytu, nietylko, że wielu się z nami zadawają, ale także wśród nas samych są wielcy ludzie.

Trochę zamieszania spowodował artykuł o Żabotyńskim. Niektórym się spodobał, mówili: ładnie napisany, a niektórym się nie spodobał, mówili: owszem, artykuł jest ładnie napisany, ale treść! Niektórzy uskarżali się na brak artykułów polityczno-aktualnych, na brak wiadomości ze świata. Niektórym nie spodobały się pojedyncze artykuły. Całość znalazła uznanie.

Stopniowo przestano mówić o gazetce. „Wszystko mija na tym bożym świecie". Znikło zainteresowanie pierwszym numerem „Frontu Uczniowskiego", miejmy nadzieję, że zdobędzie je 2-gi numer. Znowu czasem mówić, znowu będzie urozmaicenie w naszym życiu uczniowskim. Redakcja ma zamiar nas tak często niepokoić.

P. *Lewinówna* (kl. VI)

Dziewięć numerów.

Dzisiejszy numer „Frontu Uczniowskiego" jest nume em dziesiątym, jubileuszowym, należy więc zrobić bilans jego dotychczasowej działalności. Został on założony w grudniu 1935 roku i w ciągu tych dwu i pół lat wyszło już 9 numerów, których objętość wynosi ogółem 158 stronic. Z tego w r. szk. 1935/36 wydano 4 numery zawierające 66 stronic (41,1%); w r. szk. 1936/37— 3 numery objętości 56 stronic (36,1%); w r. szk. 1937/38 — dotychczas 2 numery o 36 stronicach (22,8%)— prócz niniejszego.

W tych 9 numerach wydrukowano 219 artykułów: wspomnień i wrażeń z wycieczek 51 (23,3%), artykułów o życiu samorządowym 42 (19,2%), o wielkich ludziach doby obecnej 19 (8,6%), o życiu w klasie 16 (7,3%), utworów literackich prozą 15 (6,8%), przekładów wierszy 15 (6,8%) (z hebrajskiego 5, z rosyjskiego 4, z francuskiego 3, z łaciny 2, z niemieckiego 1), własnych wierszy 12 (5,5%), artykułów treści historycznej 8 (3,9%) o literaturze i ortografii 7 (3,2%), o książkach 7 (3,2%), o wychowaniu 5 (2,3%), o muzyce 5 (2,3%), o sprawach społecznych i polityce 4 (1,8%), o sporcie 3 (1,3%), o kinie i teatrze 3 (1,3%) i innych 7 (3,2%).

Na łamach „Frontu" urządzono także 2 konkursy. Zamieszczono też 31 ilustracyj i 3 mapy.

W r. szk. 1935/36 napisało do „Frontu" 56 ucz.; w r. szk. 1936/37 — 37 ucz.; a w r. szk. 1937 38 — 29 ucz. Ten spadek tłumaczy się mniejszą ilością numerów wydanych w ostatnich dwu latach oraz zmniejszeniem się ilości ucz. niższych klas, piszących do „Frontu". W r. szk. 1935/36 z klas I napisało artykuły 11 osób, a w latach szkolnych 1936 37 i 1934 38 po 1 osobie. Ogółem w latach 1935—1938 napisało do naszej gazety 122 uczniów, z tego z kl. I 13 (10,7%), z kl. II 20 (16,4%), z kl. III 10 (8,2%), z kl. IV 21 (17,2%), z kl. I lic. 34 (27,9%), z kl. VIII 24 (19,5%).

Widzimy więc, że „Front Uczniowski" cieszy się wielką popularnością wśród uczniów, a wyniki jego dotychczasowej działalności na polu literackim i samorządowym w naszym gimnazjum są wcale pokaźne. Jeżeli więc nie ustaniemy w dalszej pracy i podwoimy wysiłki w tym kierunku za kilka lat będziemy mieli „Front Uczniowski" nie 3—4 razy do roku, lecz co miesiąc.

J. Merlis (kl. IIb)

Doc. 11. The article of P. Lewinowna about publication of the first issue of "Student Forum".

Doc. 12. The article of J.Merlis "Nine issues of "Student Forum".

Włodzimierz Żabotyński.

Włodzimierz Żabotyński obchodzi obecnie 55-tą rocznicę urodzin. A wszak ten „spiritus movens" odrodzenia narodu żydowskiego wykazuje wciąż nieustającą energję i działalność, jaką rzadko który młodzieniec w sile wieku mógłby się popisać. Zawsze ten sam, zawsze ruchliwy, produktywny—Żabotyński się nie starzeje. Wychodzi on daleko poza ramy publicysty, mówcy lub działacza partyjnego. Mało, że w każdej z wyżej wymienionych kategoryj osiągnął szczyty—posiada w sobie coś, co zmusza najzaciętszego przeciwnika politycznego do mimowolnego uznania jego nieprzeciętności. I to jest najcenniejsze w Żabotyńskim, jego osobistość, coś, co się nie da ściśle zdefinjować, a stanowi tajemnicę człowieka „jednego na pokolenie". Toteż można opowiadać o faktach z życia Żabotyńskiego, o jego dziełach, ale to nie odtworzy w całej pełni jego osobowości. Co jest istotne — to jego postawa rycerza żydostwa.

Jako rycerz jest bojownikiem, walczącym bronią rycerską przeciw uległości, upodleniu i niewolnictwu duszy galutu. Walczy on o państwo żydowskie, o „restitutio in integro" narodu żydowskiego.

Żabotyński ciągle nawołuje i żąda. Żąda decyzji, przewartościowania wartości, ofiary, pędu do doskonałości od jednostki i ogółu. Nikt z obcych nie biczował tak bezwzględnie, nie znalazł tylu surowych słów potępienia dla błędów i przywar żydostwa, w którego duszy pokutuje jeszcze getto. Wszelako w gniewie jego drga umiłowanie narodu. Jest rycerzem, a zarazem romantykiem. Jest w nim ogrom współczucia, litości i zrozumienia dla tych, których biczuje. Dlatego gniew jego wstrząsa, a nie pozostawia goryczy. Zawstydza, a nie odbiera nadziei.

Jest romantykiem i pisze stylem klasycznym. Krótkie, jasne zdania, nieomal że same rzeczowniki i czasowniki, bez przymiotnika. Mowa ze stali — a jednak umie ona łkać. Po okropnościach Safedu i Chebronu łkała mowa Żabotyńskiego. Jest prosty i wnikliwy, jego oderwane zdania są pełne treści, króra—wzrusza do głębi. Przebija się w niej nieuchwytna, tajemna melodja. Nie każdemu jest danem móc nastawić na nią antenę swej duszy. Kto potrafi—ten słyszy muzykę naszej przyszłości.

Jest prosty, a przecież skomplikowany. Jest subtelny, a szorstki i stanowczy. Ukrywa swą młodzieńczą, żywiołową miłość do narodu pod maską pogardy dla tłumu. On, któremu literatura rosyjska zawdzięcza przepiękne przekłady włoskich, francuskich i angielskich romantyków, którego pokarmem duchowym był Platon i Nietzsche, — on bezsprzecznie najlepszy po Herzlu feljetonista, słynny „Altalena", duchowy obywatel zarówno Aten jak Rzymu, Florencji z epoki odrodzenia, jak i Paryża—daje przykład najboleśniejszej ascezy, gdy wyrywa ze swej duszy ten cudowny, przepiękny, nieżydowski świat, zrzuca z ołtarza wszystkie bóżystwa i z ciasnym, nieustępliwym fanatyzmem obwieszcza: prawdziwy sjonista nie zna żadnego innego celu w życiu, jak tylko—Państwo żydowskie. Zajmuje się przytem Żabotyński drobiazgową pracą filologiczną, hebrajską ortografją i wymową—rekonstrukcją nazw geograficznych, zarowno w wielkich jak i małych rzeczach równie niezmordowany i twórczy. Nawet wtedy gdy zasądzony na śmierć za zorganizowanie obrony podczas pogromów siedzi w samotnej celi w Akko—nie ustaje w służbie dla narodu. Tworzy sam „historję legjonu żydowskiego", będącą zarazem pomnikiem dla jego brata duchowego, Trumpeldora, wokół którego narasta już legenda.

„Młodzież"—mówi Żabotyński—„nie jest tylko kwestją wieku". „Młodzież — to wysoki tytuł i nie wystarczy tylko się urodzić, by nań, zasłużyć. Nie wielka liczba lat, to tylko rzecz arytmetyki. Są niedorostki, maluczcy duchem, karły—ale to nie jest młodzież". „Być młodym — znaczy umieć wykrzesać w sobie ideał piękna i cnoty, móc oddać się bez zastrzeżeń idei, tęsknym wzrokiem spoglądać ku odwiecznym gwiazdom". W nasz ponury świat gospodarczej gmatwaniny i egoistycznych dążeń wnosi Żabotyński podniosły patos ideału, poezji i kultu narodowego.

S. Zalkind (kl. VIII).

Jak się uczyli współcześni pisarze polscy.

Wybaczcie, że zajmę się znowu takim oklepanym tematem, jak szkoła. Tym razem nie chodzi już o nas, ale o szkołę wybitnych współczesnych pisarzy polskich. Materjału dostarczyła mi ankieta, przeprowadzona przez „Wiadomości Literackie" w 1926 i 1936 r. na temat: Jak się uczyli współcześni, wybitni pisarze polscy?

Jest to naprawdę bardzo ciekawy problem, jak się odnosili oni do literatury? Pomyślicie zapewne, że od najmłodszych lat wykazywali zdol-

— z boku. Teraz napisz dwa pi er do kwadratu.— Koło kreski? — Tak. Teraz to podkreśl. —Już.— Pod tem napisz trochę na prawo znak mnożenia. Teraz napisz a — postaw nad nią trochę na prawo dwójkę, teraz napisz plus. — Wyżej czy niżej? — pośrodku! — Teraz napisz koło plusa duże N. — N czy M? — En, En! Podkreśl to. a pod kreską napisz X.

Sądzę, że każdy zdaje sobie sprawę z wiadomości matematycznych Tuwima. Tak dużo

Juljan Tuwim do „Frontu Uczniowskiego".

Doc. 14. The letter by Polish poet Julius Tuwim published in the "Students Forum"

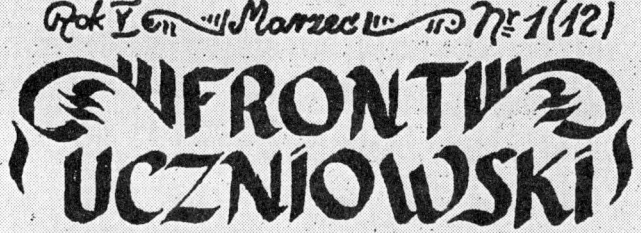

Doc.15. Front page of the report "The Robespierre Trial"

— 209 —

Odwiedzamy szkoły...

My, którzy mamy stosunkowo dobre warunki życiowe, mieszkamy w ciepłych i dużych pokojach, uczymy się w jasnych klasach, powinniśmy jednak pomyśleć o tym, że jest wiele dzieci, które tego wszystkiego nie mają. Warunki, w których żyją i uczą się, są naprawdę godne litości. Do tych dzieci należą przede wszystkim uczniowie żydowskich szkół powszechnych, a więc Szolema Alejchema, Dinenzona, szkoły dla niedorozwiniętych i chederu. Tym to właśnie szkołom powinniśmy pomóc. A przedtem musimy coś o nich wiedzieć. I w tym celu zostałyśmy wydelegowane przez zarząd naszej klasy do tych szkół, a cośmy tam widziały i poznały, niżej opiszemy.

Zaczynamy od chederu. Na bramie wisi stary, zardzewiały szyld: „Żydowska szkoła religijna". Wchodzimy na podwórze. Jest duże. Mieszczą się wokół niego dwie synagogi, a za nimi znajduje się parterowy domek. Tu mieści się cheder. Uczą się tu synowie ubogich rodziców. Przez połowę dnia ślęczą tu nad Torą, Miszną i Gemorą chłopcy różnego wieku. Większość ich ma twarze blade i wynędzniałe. Są oni jak gdyby przygnębieni. Rzadko się ich odwiedza, dla tego przybycie nasze było dla nich nowością.

Przychodzimy do szkoły „Szolema Alejchema".

Wielu z nas zna tę szkołę, lecz mało kto bliżej się nią zainteresował (wyłączając oczywiście naszą I liceralną). Dlatego też postaramy się wam ją opisać jak najdokładniej.

Lokal szkoły mieści się na drugim piętrze. Jest on nędzny. Wchodzimy na górę. Już z daleka słyszymy gwar. To dzieci wracają do domów. Przypatrzyliśmy się im uważnie. Są to dzieci różnego wyglądu i wieku. Lecz wszystkie są tak samo biedne i blade. Noszą ubrania poniszczone. Prawie nigdzie nie można dostrzec porządnie ubranego dziecka. Wszyscy są z rejonu Nowogródzkiej. Mają rodziców biednych, którzy nie mogą się nimi zająć, gdyż muszą pracować. Dzieci te mieszkają w jednopokojowych mieszkaniach. i nie mają, gdzie odrabiać lekcje. Dlatego też zeszyty ich nie mogą być czyste. Śpią często we dwójkę lub w trójkę w jednym łóżku. Czasem są oni tak biedni, że nie mają pieniędzy na jedzenie nie mówiąc już o zeszytach i książkach. Czas spędzony w szkole jest dla nich może najmilszym. Powiedźcie sami, czy nie powinniśmy się o nie zatroszczyć. Czy możemy pozwolić, żeby tyle dzieci żyło w takich warunkach.

Lecz na tym jeszcze nie koniec. Opiszemy wam także szkołę dla niedorozwiniętych. Mieści się ona przy ul. Orzeszkowej. Wchodzimy na podwórze. Dzieci pokazują nam mały budynek. To szkoła dla niedorozwiniętych. Wchodzimy i prosimy o informacje. Nauczyciele przyjmują nas bardzo życzliwie. Opowiadają nam o dziejach tej szkoły. Została ona założona w 1932 roku. A więc niedawno. Lecz mniejsza o szkołę. Nas obchodzą uczniowie. Są to przeważnie dzieci biedne i defektywne. A więc niektórzy bardzo powoli czytają, inni znów boją się wszystkiego. Lecz są wśród nich tacy, którzy są zdolni np. do malarstwa i muzyki. Pokazywano nam ich wypracowania na temat „Mój

pierwszy dzień w szkole". Jedni pisali bardzo niewyraźnie, inni powtarzali te same zwroty. Na ogół jednak wypracowania były zupełnie porządne i zaciekawiły nas bardzo.

Zapytaliśmy się o ich program nauczania. Poinformowano nas, że jest on taki sam, co w szkołach powszechnych, tylko przerabia się go o dwa la a dłużej. W klasie jest 15 uczniów, których się uczy indywidualnie. Nauczyciele które im nasze gimnazjum podarowało. Prosili, jeżeliby było możliwym, o rękawiczki. Obiecaliśmy im ich dostarczyć.

Teraz, gdy już wszyscy coś niecoś wiecie o naszych biednych, chorych kolegach, zrozumiecie, że trzeba im koniecznie pośpieszyć z pomocą. A im prędzej, tym lepiej.

§ Goldmanówna i Ł. Mazurówna

Doc. 16. The article "Visiting schools" by Lila Mazorowna and S. Goldmanowna.

Żyć to nie znaczy iść przez róże...

Żyć to nie znaczy iść przez róże
I sen z czarownej bajki śnić —
To ciągle dążyć hen ku górze
I szczęście razem z bólem wić.

To znaczy w samotności szlochać —
Przy ludziach się serdecznie śmiać,
To — ponad wszystko coś ukochać
I życie swe w ofiarę dać.

To — ból niezmierny w sercu nosić
Lub szare, smutne pędzić dni,
Minione szczęście łzami rosić,
Gdy nowe się jedynie śni!

To — kiedy czasem ciężko będzie
I z piersi twej się wydrze jęk —
Nie mówić, że to śpiew łabędzi,
Że to ostatni życia dźwięk.

To — ciągle walczyć, bić się z losem,
Do zmagań w sobie wzbudzić żar,
Nie cofać się przed ciężkim ciosem,
Uwierzyć w cenny życia dar.

To — naprzód ciągle iść, padając,
Ku dalekiemu słońcu hen!
Sobie wszystkiego odmawiając,
Wywalczyć przyszłym szczęścia sen.

I trzeba umieć z szarych nitek
Tkaniny tkać, co złotem lśnią,
I w jeden piękny upleść zwitek
Te struny, które w sercu drżą.

Żyć to nie znaczy iść przez róże
I sen z czarownej bajki śnić —
To wciąż padając iść ku górze —
Cierpieć — kochając — znaczy żyć.

R. Fajnówna (kl. VI).

Doc. 17 "To live does not mean to walk through roses."
Poem by R. Fajnowna.

Doc. 18. Essay
"YIVO Institute
for Jewish Research"

II. Żydowski Instytut Naukowy
(I. W. O.)

Chcąc zapoznać swych czytelników z działalnością Żydowskiego Instytutu Naukowego, redakcja „F. U." wysłała mnie do tej instytucji w celu dokonania wywiadu z dr. Maksem Weinreichem. Już na samym progu oryginalnego budynku uderza mnie duża mapa ścienna, ilustrująca rozmieszczenie 16-miljonowej masy żydowskiej na całym świecie w r. 1934. Obok mieszczą się wykresy, przedstawiające działalność Ż. I. N.u.

Przyjmuje mnie bardzo uprzejmie dr. Weinreich, jeden z najwybitniejszych działaczy żydowskich, do którego kieruję szereg pytań.

— Kiedy i w jaki sposób Ż. I. N. został utworzony?

— Za właściwą datę powstania tej instytucji uważa się 24 marca 1925 r. Twórcą tego projektu był wybitny działacz żydowski N. Sztif, który bawił wówczas w Berlinie. Projektem jego zajęli się inni działacze, jak Czirikower, Rejzin, Leszczyński i ja.

— Jakie ważniejsze momenty zaznaczyły się w rozwoju Ż. I. N.u?

— Instytut zaczął prawie od niczego, a w ciągu kilku lat niezmiernie się rozrósł. Pierwsze posiedzenia odbywały się w mojem prywatnem mieszkaniu, wnet jednak zajął pokój w domu przy ul. W. Pohulanki 18, a potem drugi, aż wreszcie całe piętro. W r. 1933 przeniósł się do własnego budynku przy ul. Wiwulskiego 18.

— W r. 1925 odbyła się pierwsza większa narada w Berlinie, a w 1929 pierwsza konferencja w Wilnie. Ważną datą w dziejach Ż. I. N.u jest rok 1931, kiedy wydano pierwsze pismo p. n. „Iwo-bleter."

— Jakie cele wytknął sobie Instytut?

— Ż. I. N. ma się stać ośrodkiem naukowej pracy żydowskiej i instytucją, wychowującą młodych pracowników naukowych.

— Jaka jest organizacja pracy naukowej?

— Instytut tworzy 4 sekcje: filologiczną, ekonomiczno-statystyczną, historyczną i psychologiczno-pedagogiczną. Zorganizowano ponadto badanie młodzieży żyd. w wieku 16 — 20 lat. W tym celu przeprowadzono konkursową ankietę autobiograficzną. Prócz głównych sekcyj czynne są jeszcze pomocnicze, jak centrala bibljograficzna, archiwum, bibljoteka i muzeum.

P. dr. Weinreich demonstruje mi również wykres organizacji Ż. I. N.u, na którym widać jak koła zbieraczy łączą się w stowarzyszenia, te zaś tworzą już organizacje krajowe, mające prawo wysyłania delegatów na ogólny zjazd. Ten wyłania ze siebie kuratorjum, radę i zarząd centralny, który znowu tworzy biuro wykonawcze. W skład prezydjum honorowego wchodzą takie osobistości, jak Einstein, Dubnow, Freud i in.

P. dr. Weinreich proponuje mi zwiedzanie gmachu, na co skwapliwie się godzę. Oglądam istny labirynt, a więc muzeum teatralne, centralę bibljograficzną, czytelnie, podziemne magazyny, aż dotarliśmy do wystawy, obrazującej życie i twórczość „Mendele Mojcher Sforim".

— Jak się przedstawia bibljoteka i zbiory Instytutu?

— Bibljoteka liczy 40000 tomów, prócz 10000 roczników żyd. czasopism, 350 autobiografij, 100000 pieśni, legend, przysłowi i opisów zwyczajów ludowych, 2000 objektów, tyczących się teatrów, autorów i dramaturgów żyd. A wszystko to pochodzi wyłącznie z darów.

— Z jakich powodów i w jakim celu odbył się ostatni zjazd Ż. I. N.-u?

— W r. 1935 odbył się ogólny zjazd po 6-letniej przerwie. Zadaniem jego było - wysłuchać sprawozdania z dotychczasowej działalności Instytutu, wybrać nowy zarząd centralny i uchwalić dlań dyrektywy. Między innemi uchwalono rozszerzyć aspiranturę im. C. Szabada. Prof. Dubnow przyrzekł kierować pracą aspirantów na polu badań historycznych. Aby umożliwić młodym adeptom nauki całkowite poświęcenie się studjom, Ż. I. N. udziela im stypendjów.

— Z jakich funduszów utrzymuje się Ż. I. N.?

— Z ofiar różnych towarzystw i instytucyj na całym świecie. Budżet Instytutu wynosi pół miljona złotych rocznie, z tego trzecią część pokrywają St. Zj. A. P., drugie miejsce zajmuje Polska, a za nią idzie reszta krajów.

— Jakie są nowe zamierzenia Ż. I. N-u ?

— Ukończono obecnie przygotowania do założenia muzeum sztuki żydowskiej.

Na tem podziękowawszy p. dr. Weinreichowi za jego uprzejme i wyczerpujące informacje, opuszczam budynek Ż. I. N-u.

S. Floksówna (kl. VIII).

Z działalności Żyd. Instytutu Muzycznego w Wilnie.

Żydowski Instytut Muzyczny został założony w roku 1925 z inicjatywy Żydowskiego Stowarzyszenia Krzewienia Sztuki.

Założenie tej placówki kulturalnej miało ogromne znaczenie dla społeczeństwa żydowskiego. Dotychczas bowiem ludności żydowskiej nie miała własnej instytucji muzycznej, a przeciętny człowiek nie mógł sobie pozwolić na wyjazd do większego miasta dla studjów muzycznych. Ż. I. M. właśnie miał temu zaradzić.

Na dyrektora Instytutu wybrano Rafała Rubinsztejna, człowieka bardzo zdolnego, a przytem energicznego i przedsiębiorczego. Pomagają mu zaś dzielnie osoby, którym zależy na istnieniu tej instytucji.

Ż. I. M. zajmuje się nietylko pracą pedagogiczną, ale stara się także udostępnić muzykę operową szerszym masom żydowskim. W pierwszych latach swego istnienia Ż. I. M. wystawił operę „Trawiatę" Verdiego dzięki wysiłkom dyr. Rubinsztejna. Wystawił on po raz pierwszy w Polsce operę w jęz. żydowskim, budząc tem zainteresowanie u społeczeństwa żydowskiego. Po „Trawiacie" przyszła kolej na inne opery.

MÓJ SEN.

Naogół śni mi się bardzo rzadko. Jeśli zaś miewam kiedy sny, to w większości wypadków nie pozostaje po nich żaden ślad. Widziadła senne szybko mi się zacierają w pamięci i przy największym nawet wysiłku nie jestem ich w sta nie odtworzyć. Jeden jedyny raz miałam w życiu sen, który zapamiętałam dokładnie. Było to podczas świąt Sukot. Godzina 11 w nocy. Pokój mój zalega martwa cisza, przerywana raz poraz tykaniem zegara. Leżę w łóżku i czytam jeden z rozdziałów pięknej, utopijnej powieści L. Belmonta p. t. „Ziemia obiecana". Wielka wskazówka zegara rozpędziła się za małą, aby się z nią spotkać na dwunastce. Powoli przestaję czytać. Zamiast słów przesuwają mi się przed oczyma obrazy piękne, zaklęte w stronicach tej czarującej powieści. Zaczynam śnić na jawie. Wtem — bęc! Książka mi wypadła z rąk. Gaszę lampę. Anioł snu przymyka mi powieki. Dobranoc.

Jak błogo! Triest. W porcie ożywiony ruch. Tysiąc młodych ludzi, między nimi i ja, zaległo molo pasażerskie. Za godzinę ruszamy w drogę do Erec! Zawiezie nas tam okręt „Tel-Awiw", na którego maszcie powiewa biało-niebieska chorągiew. Gwizd syreny.

Wsiadać! — rozlega się głos kapitana.

W okamgnieniu molo opustoszało.

„Hakszejw"! — przeszyło nagle powietrze. Tysiąc młodych ciał się wyprężyło. Orkiestra gra Hatikwę. Włosi salutują. Okręt drgnął. Odjazd.

Pogoda piękna. Krajobraz czarujący: południowe niebo, błogi wietrzyk. Okręty w porcie maleją coraz bardziej, już wyglądają, jak zabawki. Dziób „Tel-Awiwu" rozpruwa fale morskie. Na pokładzie wesoło: śpiew, pląsy i znowu pląsy i znowu śpiew. Tańczę, śpiewam, ale myśli moje mkną daleko... hen daleko... do Erec.

Okręt mknie raźno naprzód, przejęty upojną pieśnią nadziei, śpiewaną przez fale morskie wracającym z wiekowej tułaczki wygnańcom.

Chajfa! Nieprzebrane tłumy na molu. Śpiew, muzyka, nawoływania — wszystko to oszałamia mię. Ludzie padają sobie w objęcia. Niektórzy płaczą z radości. A ja! Porwana w objęcia brata, zaczęłam łkać. Nim się zdołałam opanować, już siedziałam w taksówce. Jechałam idealnie gładką szosą, budowaną przez chaluców. Przez szybę miałam widok na okolicę. Jak w kinie przesuwają mi się przed oczyma cudowne obrazy kolonij, tonących w morzu zieleni i w złotych blaskach słońca palestyńskiego. Ogarnęło mnie wkrótce znużenie. Zasnęłam, mając głowę opartą o ramię brata. Kiedy nagle... wzdrygnęłam się...

Katastrofa? Nie, broń Boże! To mama mnie szarpnęła za rękaw.

„Wstawaj dziecko" rzekła „za 15 siódma. Spóźnisz się do szkoły".

Co? Szkoła? Spóźnisz się? Gdzie ja właściwie jestem? Czyżby to miał być sen?

Przecieram oczy. Tak, nic innego. Na podłodze leży „Ziemia obiecana", sprawczyni czarownego snu.

P. *Dajchesówna* (kl. IIa).

KOEDUK. SZKOŁA POWSZECHNA Z POLSKIM JĘZYKIEM NAUCZANIA
PRZY HUMANISTYCZNEM GIMNAZJUM Z PEŁNEMI PRAWAMI GIMN. PAŃSTWOWYCH
C. EPSZTEJNA i J. SZPAJZERA
W WILNIE

Nr. 10   Rok szkolny 1932/33

ŚWIADECTWO SZKOLNE

urodzona *Himelfarbówna Rywka* dnia *16 czerwca* 1924 r. w *Wilnie*
(powiat:), religji (wyznania) *mojż.*
uczenica oddziału *trzeciego*

otrzymuje za rok szkolny 1932/33 stopnie następujące:

ze sprawowania się	bardzo dobry
z nauki religji	dobry
„ języka polskiego	dobry
„ języka	
„ rachunków z geometrją	dobry
„ przyrody	dobry
„ geografji	dobry
„ historji	dobry
„ rysunków	dobry
„ robót ręcznych	dobry
„ śpiewu	dobry
„ ćwiczeń cielesnych	dobry
„ robót kobiecych	

Liczba opuszczonych godzin szkolnych *130* z czego nie usprawiedliwiono /
Liczba spóźnień /. z czego nie usprawiedliwiono

Wynik ogólny *dobry*

Wilnie, dnia *14 czerwca* 1933 r.

Opiekun(ka) oddziału   Kierownik szkoły

Doc. 20 Diploma of Rywka Himelfarbowna

PRYWATNE
GIMNAZJUM KOEDUKACYJNE
C. Epsztejna i L. Szpajzera
w WILNIE

E. Ka

Egzamin z języka polskiego

Opiszę pamiętne zdarzenie z mego życia.

Było to dwa lata temu. Jak zwykle, po zwolnieniu nas ze szkoły pojechałem na letnisko. Gospodarz naszego letniska miał syna, córkę, i psa. Od pierwszego dnia zaprzyjaźniłem się z niemi. Kochałem ich bardzo, ale oni mnie też. Najwięcej kochaliśmy naszego nieodłączonego przyjaciela: psa Burka. Jak tylko był ranek, nasz pies budził nas, szczekając po poświutku.

Gdzie tylko szliśmy, szedł pies z nami, który nam drogę. Był dla nas najlepszym psem na świecie. Ale nie długo trwało to szczęście. W naszej okolicy zjawił się wściekły pies, który pokąsał kilka psów. Policja, dowiedziawszy się o tym zdarzeniu, zaczęła strzelać psów. Gdy doszła do nas ta wieść, schowaliśmy naszego Burka do stodoły. Gdy policja weszła na nasze podwórko, Burek, czując jakby obcych ludzi, czyhających na jego śmierć, zaczął szczekać! Kazano otworzyć stodołę i ztąd rozlegało się szczekanie psa. Pies wybiegł ztamtąd jak szalony. Po chwili padł ten strzał. Nasz Burek zabity. Na widok leżącego psa rozpłakaliśmy się. Z bólem w sercu wróciłem do miasta. Jeszcze teraz, gdy wspomnę o Burku łzy mi stoją w oczach, gdy wiem, że ci przyszli zabili psa cudzemi rękoma.

Doc. 21. The test work by E. Kantorowicz

Nr kolejny 23		
Jakub Merlis		
urodzony dnia 13-go czerwca 1924 r. w Wilnie		
(powiat ———), religii (wyznania) mojżesz.		
uczęszczał do klasy trzeciej 8. liceum (gimnazjum) *)		
otrzymuje oceny:	Za pierwsze półrocze	Za cały rok szkolny
sprawowanie	bardzo dobry	bardzo dobry
religia	bardzo dobry	bardzo dobry
język polski	bardzo dobry	bardzo dobry
język łaciński	bardzo dobry	bardzo dobry
język grecki		
język *niemiecki*	bardzo dobry	bardzo dobry
historia	bardzo dobry	bardzo dobry
zagadnienia życia współczesnego		
geografia (geografia i geologia) ?	bardzo dobry	bardzo dobry
biologia		
fizyka i chemia (fizyka z astronomią) ?	bardzo dobry	bardzo dobry
Chemia z astronomią		
matematyka	bardzo dobry	bardzo dobry
propedeutyka filozofii		
przysposobienie wojskowe		
zajęcia praktyczne	bardzo dobry	bardzo dobry
ćwiczenia cielesne	bardzo dobry	bardzo dobry
rysunki		
Przedmioty nadobowiązkowe		
Opuścił dni szkolnych	3	18
z czego nie usprawiedliwiono		
Uchwałą Rady Pedagogicznej otrzymał promocję do klasy *czwartej*		
Data wydania świadectwa: za I półrocze 22/19.38, duplikatu		
za rok szkolny 19/VI.39, odejścia		
Uwagi:		

Doc. 22. Diploma of Jakub Merlis. All marks "excellent."

Doc. 23. Essay "My First Letter" by Zalik Rudnicki

Doc. 24. Essay "Is It Possible to Empty an Ocean?" by Tania Spektorowna

Wakacje w mieście.

Lato. To znaczy: świadectwo, upał, letnisko i woda. Lecz mojej marnej osobie nie było sądzonym opuścić Wilno. Mama wyjechała do Paryża, zaś Tato, rekin interesów, jak to się o nim jeden ze znajomych wyraził, nie ma przecież czasu na zajmowanie się takim brzdącem nieznośnym. Chcąc nie chcąc pozostałem. Lecz na moje zbawienie dowiedziałem się, że istnieje takie Ż. T. G. S. „Makabi", gdzie za opłatę 50 groszy miesięcznie, t. zn. 1¹|₂ grosza dziennie, można wylęgiwać się rozkosznie na słońcu i kąpać się w tym cudnym basenie, który choć drewniany zdaje się być stokrotnie lepszy od innych zagranicznych cementowych. Jak może szerszemu ogółowi wiadomo, mam miano filozofa klasowego. A tu znów całkiem się zmieniło: koledzy na basenie nazwali mnie „wibrą" (i to nie klasyczną).

Pierwsze dwa tygodnie przeszły dość jednostajnie, a potem wybrałem się do Grzegorzewa, gdzie znajduje s'ę słynna szkoła szybowcowa. Już od dawna starałem się o przyjęcie do niej. Wkońcu jednak udało mi się. Szkolenie, a przeważnie jego początek, nie należy do zbyt przyjemnych. „Szubienica", „skoki" itd. Z początku przyprawiały mię o mdłości, lecz po niejakim czas'e już krzepko siedziałem na „fotelu" i wymachiwałem z energią sterem. Mój pierwszy lot nadspodziewanie udał się i wróciłem do domu z kategorią „A". Za dwa lata, już w Ausztagirach zobaczycie mię jako kandydata na kategorię „B".

Drugi miesiąc przeszedł mi bardzo szybko. Częste wycieczki do kolegi w Nowych Werkach urozmaicały mi czas. Miałem tam kilka malowniczych przygód, a jedna z nich omal nie zakończyła się katastrofalnie, bo łowiąc ryby wpadłem do wody i ledwo nie dostałem się pod wodospad. Lecz dzięki memu wyszkoleniu w „Makabi" i przezwisku „żabka" wydostałem się jakoś z matni. No, a teraz mogę was zapewnić z radością i dumą, że mimo pozostawania w mieście spędziłem wakacje w niejednym wypadku barwniej i weselej od was.

J. Stołowicki (kl. IIb).

Doc. 25. The article "My Summer Vacation in the City" by Jakob Stolowicki

Egzamin z języka polskiego do klasy III gim. N. Szylańska

Spacer po mieście w godzinach wieczornych.

Po tragicznym i przytłaczającym dramacie, który oglądałam w kinie, śpieszę do domu. Jednak ulica pełna szumu i światła *[pozn.]* [...] samochodów dookoła tętni pełnią życia. Oświetlone wystawy i reklamy rzucają jaskrawe światła na ludzi spieszących się dokądś nerwowych, pałających lub skrytych w sobie. Sama się czuję mała w tym tłumie ludzi, nie wiedząc, dokąd się skierować. Słychać muzykę z otwartych okien domów, raz ostro, potem znów łagodnie, grające figlarne skoczne... Za chwilę rozpocznie się życie nocne, a piękne lemuryny będą zatrzymywać się przed kinami, gdy... ciemność zalega miasto.
Z pobliskiego domu słychać ciche uderzenia zegara wybijającego 10 uderzeń. Miasto się uspokaja, się na [...] taksze je czarną płachtą uśpione jak małe dziecko.
Żółte światła latarni rzucają smutne blaski. Kiedy wraz to wzmagając się kołysze dziecię chorem. Mały desczyk zarysza gdzieś słota, [...] teraz w lekkiej mgle naszych małych ucieków domowych, starych murami ożywają domy rzucają cień na ulicę [...] widać skrawek nieba.
Już [...] ptaków tylko czasem słychać [...] tak jakby z polskiej książki.

Doc. 26. Essay "A Walk through the Streets of Vilna during the Evening" by Noema Shilanska

PRYWATNE
GIMNAZJUM KOED. IKACYJNE
C. Epsztejna i I. Szpajzera
w WILNIE

Egzamin z j. polskiego.   J. Rafes
Opiszę pamiętne zdarzenie z mego
życia.
Działo się to na letnisku latem.
Miałem wtencas 8 lat i jako wszyscy
chłopiec w tym wieku byłem bardzo
łakomy. Lubiłem bardzo słodkie rze-
czy, a przeważnie krem. Pewnego u nas
w domu rozpuszczono płyn "Sidol" do
czyszczenia klamek i postawiono go na
stoliczku w kuchni. Zobaczywszy go w
talerzyku myślałem, że to jest krem,
pobiegłem więc do mamusi spytać
się pozwolenia lecz mamusi nie było
w domu. Pomyślałem sobie, że gdy
nie ma mamusia, nie będzie się gnie-
wać. Poszedłem więc do kuchni, wziąłem
ten rzekomy krem i spróbowałem go.
Odrazu zebrało się na wymioty i wy-
miotowałem. Gdy przyszli rodzice, bardzo się śmieli i radowali, że zostałem ukarany za moje łakomstwo,
którego skutkiem była moja dwuty-
godniowa choroba. I tak zostałem
ukarany za moje łakomstwo.

Doc. 27. Essay for a Polish test "Write about something outstanding about your life" by Julek Rafes